Fermenting

An Essential Guide to Culturing Food to Create Kombucha, Sourdough, Kimchi, Sauerkraut, Yogurt, and More so You Can Grow Probiotics at Home and Improve Your Gut Microbiome

Contents

Introduction

Gut health is an essential aspect of your overall health and well-being. However, given the modern diet and lifestyle, most people have compromised their gut health and suffer from its side effects. If you want to improve your health and get your gut biome back to its healthiest state, this is the book for you. You might have heard about fermentation and the benefits of eating fermented foods. If not, you will soon discover the wonders of fermentation. Humans have been consuming fermented foods for a long time, but people have only recently started paying more attention to this type of food. Your beer, bread, salami, etc., are all fermented foods. They all have their own unique textures and smells and are a great addition to your diet.

Probiotics are one of the best things you can put into your body, and making your own at home is an invaluable skill. As you read on, you will learn about fermentation, its history, the process, benefits, and how to ferment various foods. This book will help you learn more about probiotics and how they can improve your gut health.

Kimchi, for instance, is a great probiotic that is a staple of Korean cuisine. Koreans seem to know enough about fermentation and its various benefits because they regularly consume kimchi. Throughout this book, you will learn how to make authentic Korean Kimchi at home too. Similarly, you will soon be making your own yogurt, kombucha, sourdough, and more. Learning how to culture your food will benefit your health and that of those around you.

This fermentation guide is different from others on the market. You may have found those challenging to follow or lacking crucial information. Here you will get easy-to-understand guidelines on how you can get started with fermentation. It contains hands-on instructions to make it easy for beginners to make the best sourdough, kimchi, yogurt, etc. This book provides you with simple recipes to help you make the best fermented foods. There are variations for each recipe that should suit every taste.

So, if you are ready to start growing your own probiotics and improving your gut health, let's get started.

Chapter One: Introduction to Fermenting

First, let's familiarize you with what fermenting foods means and why it is used. We will start by giving both the historical and the cultural background to fermenting foods. You will also learn how beneficial gut bacteria can be for your health. This section discusses the three fermentation types: lactic acid fermentation, acetic acid fermentation, and alcoholic fermentation.

Fermentation is a fascinating process, and this book is all about it. Also known as culturing, the basic and most important aspect of fermentation is a microbe. These microbes are tiny organisms present all around us, including your body, soil, and home. Many people think bacteria of all types are harmful to us and cause diseases. However, some microbes are actually beneficial for the body and even protect you against various illnesses. The important thing is to have a good balance of microbes in your body.

History of Fermentation

Fermentation has been around as long as man. Its exact origins have not been determined yet, but evidence shows fermentation being used as far back as 7000 BC. In Chinese history, there is evidence they used fermentation to create rice wine around 4000 BC. The word itself comes from "fervere," a Latin word meaning "to boil." It probably referred to the conversion of fruit juice to wine after yeast was introduced to it.

Initially, our ancestors depended on fermentation for survival. They did not have easy access to food, and they needed to find ways to preserve it. They also had to prepare their rations so they could survive from one season to another.

Preserved food was especially important during winters when they couldn't grow or hunt for food as easily. They needed an option for when the harvest season had passed or when they couldn't hunt. These needs were how grapes were turned into wine and milk was made into cheese. Most countries in the world have their own traditions of fermenting food.

Egyptians made beer and bread with controlled yeast. Fruit juices were fermented to make tonics, wines, and cordials. The Romans made garum by fermenting fish guts. The Norwegians discovered the salted salmon buried and left for a while tasted different from fresh salmon but was still edible and delicious. In Russia, they left vegetable scraps in a barrel to age in winter, and this was how the original borscht was prepared. In Korea, cabbage was buried to last through the winter, resulting in the discovery of kimchi.

The western equivalent of this was sauerkraut in Europe. As our ancestors adapted to their environment and made new discoveries, they provided us with many different food options. The techniques and tools have been refined over the years, and we have better control over the process. The basics of the traditional methods lie at the core of preparing good, fermented foods. You can use accurate tools and techniques to get the desired results, but you also need to depend on your senses of taste and smell when it comes to fermentation.

In every culture, you can see traces of fermentation being passed over for generations. Humans have been using natural microbes for their health benefits for a long time. The beginnings of fermentation are unknown, but it is believed it might have started on accident. Someone might have dropped wild yeast or microbes in some grape juice, grain, or other food. This would have allowed for the fermentation process to spontaneously occur if the surrounding temperature was right. Ideally, temperatures between 40 and 70 °F can easily support fermentation.

The benefits of fermented foods have led people to embrace the process for a long time. In the next chapter, you will learn more about why fermentation is important and how it is beneficial. Many different techniques vary from culture to culture.

For instance, dairy farmers used fermentation to store milk for longer by turning it into cheese. Cheese is one of the earliest and most basic fermented products we know of. The core ingredients used for fermentation vary according to what was available in certain places. It could simply be dependent on what local microbes liked to consume.

The fermentation of certain foods is usually referred to as culture. This is because cultures or communities of microbes colonize a food. These microbes use the naturally occurring sugars in food for energy and simultaneously cause the fermentation process in food. This process takes place without the presence of oxygen and is thus called anaerobic digestion. It results in the creation of products like kombucha, cheese, sauerkraut, etc.

Wine, leavened bread, and beer are some of the earliest fermented foods. East Asian fermented foods like kimchi, pickles, vinegar, yogurt, etc., soon followed. In recent times, fermentation is also used for making vitamins B-12 and B-2, antibiotics, gluconic acid, and citric acid. Modern industrial fermentations also create microalgae and nutritional yeast.

In ancient times, the process of fermentation was somewhat of a marvel and mystery to humans. They did not really understand what caused or allowed fermentation to occur, and some even attributed it to the work of divine forces. In Japan, early breweries often had a small shrine where daily prayers were offered. In Greek mythology, Bacchus was proclaimed the god of wine.

One of the most significant contributors to the science of fermentation was Louis Pasteur. He was a French chemist and physicist who made discoveries that left a lasting impact on science, including the subject of fermentation. His germ theory, the Pasteurization method, and the creation of vaccines are some of the most significant contributions to science.

Around 1856, he connected fermentation to yeast, which made him the first zymologist in the world. An accident took place in a sugar beetroot distillery, and he was asked to investigate it. He discovered the spoiled batch had high levels of lactic acid instead of alcohol, which was why it tasted sour. The sour batch had a large amount of lactic acid bacteria, and this observation played a fundamental role in what we now know about the role of bacteria and fungi in fermentation. His observations allowed him to understand that the process took place in an anaerobic environment.

Later, Eduard Buechner discovered that fermentation could also occur with cell-free yeast extracts driven only by their enzymes. Fermented foods were considered a health benefit only around 1910. At this point, Elie Metchnikoff, a Russian bacteriologist, determined that Bulgarians have a longer lifespan than others because their diet had a larger amount of fermented milk. Over the last few decades, more research has been conducted to study and understand fermentation. This research has shown a clear link between improved digestion and friendly bacteria. Therefore, probiotics became a widely recommended part of the diet.

What Is Fermentation?

It is a process where organic substances are chemically transformed into simpler compounds due to the action of enzymes produced by bacteria, yeast, and other microorganisms. The enzymes break down complex organic molecules into smaller compounds and nutrients. In the case of food, fermentation makes the end product more digestible for humans and creates distinct texture, aroma, and flavor, which improve the initial product. Fermentation processes are usually activated by yeasts, molds, or bacteria, either in groups or singularly.

All microorganisms have their own unique metabolic genes, and these produce enzymes that will break down specific types of sugar metabolites. In the process of fermentation, different kinds of microbes are present in various proportions. They work together to give you your desired fermented byproduct. The taste of certain fermented foods will vary depending on the numbers and types of microbes used in the process.

Various Types of Fermentation

• Alcoholic Fermentation

Yeasts break down pyruvate molecules in sugars and convert them to alcohol. The most well-known kind of fermentation is alcoholic fermentation. The byproducts in the form of wine, beer, etc., have been enjoyed by humans for thousands of years.

• Acetic Acid Fermentation

Sugars from fruit or grains are converted to sour vinegar and other condiments. This process starts when alcoholic fermentation ends. Vinegar is the most common byproduct of acetic acid fermentation. This is why apple cider is different from apple cider vinegar.

• Lactic Acid Fermentation

Sugars or starches are broken down, and lactic acid is produced. This is considered the oldest method of fermentation. Fermented milk products are found in most cultures worldwide, and these have been consumed for centuries.

When you start working on fermenting your foods, you must remember that it is essentially a sort of controlled decay. Fermentation leads to the creation of intense flavors and aromas that might be appealing to some and not to others. Such foods are not fresh, but they aren't rotten either. The consumption of fermented foods is a way to improve the digestion of other foods and create an unsuitable environment for undesirable bacteria in the body. The type of fermented food you consume will depend on your taste. Use this guide to try a few different fermentations and see what suits your palate. Add these to your diet for their health benefits and also as a way to waste less food.

Popular Fermented Foods

Some popular fermented foods in this guide include:

- **Kimchi and Sauerkraut**

Kimchi is a Korean side dish that is made by fermenting vegetables like radish and cabbage. Typically, kimchi contains radish or cabbage with chili, garlic, pepper, ginger, green onion, and salt. Other ingredients like pear and apple may also be used. There are substantial amounts of Leuconostoc bacteria in it, and these produce lactic acid. Sauerkraut is made by fermenting cabbage and was originally from Northern China but may have been brought by the Mongols to Europe. It can be wild fermented or made with a starter culture. In wild fermented versions, you will find high levels of Pseudomonas and Enterobacter. In sauerkraut with a starter culture, there are higher levels of Lactobacillus, Leuconostoc, and Pediococcus.

- **Miso**

It is a popular Japanese paste obtained through the fermentation of mashed soybeans, grains, and salt. This richly fermented bean paste is made with Aspergillus oryzae, which is a type of mold. While any legume or even a mixture of legumes can be used, soybeans are the popular choice.

- **Cheese**

Cheese is one of the earliest fermented products, made from fermented milk, and is produced by the coagulation of casein, a milk protein. During the process of fermentation, microbes like lactic acid-producing bacteria acidify the milk. Enzymes like rennet then coagulate the milk. After the dairy solids are separated, they are pressed down into certain shapes, and they then go through the process of aging. This promotes the growth of molds in the cheese. The cheese's flavor, color, texture, and aroma are determined by the type of milk, environmental factors, and the types of mold and bacteria involved in the fermentation process. Probiotic starter cultures usually initiate cheese production, but the bacteria don't always survive the lengthy aging process. In cheeses like cheddar and Gouda, small numbers of probiotic bacteria survive and will be present in the final cheese product.

- **Kombucha**

It is believed that kombucha originated around 220 BC in China, Eastern Europe, or Russia. The fermentation of green or black tea gives you this healthy drink. It is slightly alcoholic and effervescent. The mixture of sugar and tea acts as a fermentation medium for the symbiotic culture of yeast and bacteria in a rubbery disk shape. This is a biofilm of many microbes like Komagataeibacter xylinus and Zygosaccharomyces bailii. Spices, fruit, and juices are also added to kombucha for flavor. Jun kombucha is a variation of the drink where green tea and honey are used as a medium for fermentation. The honey provides additional probiotic benefits to the kombucha.

Traditionally prepared kombucha is more beneficial than the processed ones available in stores these days.

• Mead

Honey and water are fermented to produce mead. It can also include spices, fruits, or grains.

• Natto

Natto is another Japanese fermented dish. It is made from soybeans and has an intense aroma and flavor. The soybean is fermented with Bacillus subtilis var. natto. It is usually eaten with breakfast.

• Kefir

Kefir originated from the Caucasus Mountains and is a fermented milk product. Kefir grains made of bacteria, sugars, lipids, proteins, and yeast are used for fermentation. A symbiotic microbial culture is created when the yeast and bacteria feed on the nutrients present in the grains. Milk from goats, cows, or sheep can be used to make kefir. It gives a sour and effervescent product that is good for the gut.

• Tempeh

Cooked soybeans are fermented to produce this cake-like form that is good for digestion. It is traditionally an Indonesian dish made by boiling, dehulling and fermenting soybeans. Usually, a starter culture of a type of mold called Rhizopus oligosporus is used to make tempeh.

• Chocolate

The seeds from the Theobroma cacao tree are fermented to make chocolate. This tree is native to the Amazon rainforest but grows elsewhere as well. The cacao pods from the tree are harvested, and the pulp and seed are left to ferment. The microbes that participate in this fermentation include Acetobacter pasteurianus, Lactobacillus fermentum, S. cerevisiae, Hortaea thailandica, Pichia kudriavzevii, and Hanseniaspora opuntiae. The first two are bacteria, while the rest are yeast species. During the drying and roasting of the beans, most of these microbes are killed. Many bioactive microbes remain, and these are responsible for the aroma and flavor of chocolate.

- **Yogurt**

Yogurt is obtained from the fermentation of acidified milk and thickened using probiotic species like Streptococcus thermophilus and Lactobacillus bulgaricus. This fermented food has been consumed for thousands of years. The term yogurt was coined from "yogurmak," a Turkish word that means coagulate. Ancient Ayurvedic texts contain mentions of yogurt and its health benefits as well. This fermented product can be produced from the milk of many different animals like goats, cows, camels, and yaks. Yogurt was even sold as a medicinal substance at the beginning of the 20th century. Yogurt production in the food industry became more common after the Danone yogurt factory was established in France in 1932.

- **Sourdough Bread**

Throughout history, bread was primarily made with the help of sourdough fermentation. Quick rise bread and industrial yeast were not invented until later. This transition to the latter meant that we now consume bread that is harder for the body to digest and is filled with antinutrients. For sourdough bread, a starter is created and mixed with water and flour. This is left out at room temperature for a few days. The lactic acid-producing bacteria in the air and yeast will colonize the starter and initiate the fermentation. There are no active probiotic cultures in sourdough bread, but it has a lower glycemic index and other benefits compared to modern bread.

- **Beer**

Beer is produced using a starch source, water, and yeast. Usually, some cereal grains are steeped in water, and the liquid is then fermented using yeast. Grains have to be malted before they can be fermented for producing beer. The cereal grains germinate during malting and release enzymes that will break down complex carbs present in the grains into simple sugar. The yeast feeds on the simple sugars and then produces alcohol. Hops and brewer's yeast are used to ferment most types of beers. Beer is, in fact, the most widely consumed alcohol and fermented drink in the world.

Chapter Two: Why Fermentation Is Important

In this chapter, you will understand why fermentation is an essential aspect of overall health. It underlines the importance of bacteria in the human body. You will soon see how devoid your food supply is of vital nutrients due to commercial farming and pesticide use. It is important to be aware of the damaging results of fast-food diets and the use of antibiotics in farming. Eating fermented foods can improve the absorption of vital nutrients, provide a healthy gut microbiome and build a stronger immune system.

Why Fermented Foods Are Good for You

You may be wondering why fermented foods are good for you. The answer is bioactive compounds. The probiotic content in fermented foods is usually responsible for all their benefits. Not every fermented food contains viable probiotics. Despite this, even fermented foods that lack those probiotics are beneficial for your health because of the various bioactive compounds found in fermented foods.

- **Bioactive Peptides**

Bioactive peptides are produced by certain lactic acid-producing bacteria that are present in fermented foods. These bioactive peptides are small organic molecules that are joined by peptide bonds. Some bioactive peptides like bacteriocins are antimicrobial in nature.

- **Phenolic Compounds**

These are small molecules that have a ring-shaped chemical group called phenol. Polyphenols are phenolic compounds present in blueberries, blackberries, and other colorful fruits. Fermentation increases some phenolic compounds with antioxidant properties that also balance the microbiome in the gut.

- **Prebiotics and Micronutrients**

Fermented foods act as a bioavailable delivery system for micronutrients and prebiotics like calcium.

- **Easier Digestibility**

Compounds that are usually difficult to digest for the body are broken down through fermentation. This includes FODMAPs in grains, vegetables, and legumes, as well as the lactose in dairy.

Benefits of Fermented Foods

- **Improves Gut Health**

The first and most important benefit of fermented foods is that they support the gut microbiome. Many studies have been conducted to understand how the gut is affected by the consumption of fermented foods. Kefir is a fermented milk product that increases the concentration of friendly bacteria like Lactococcus, Lactobacillus, and Bifidobacteria in the gut, thus benefiting it. The consumption of tempeh will increase the concentration of Akkermansia muciniphila. It also increases immunoglobulin A levels, which is important for immune response in the intestines. Chocolate supplies prebiotic fibers and short-chain fatty acids that support beneficial microbes in the gut as well.

• Better Bowel Regulation

Healthy bowel movements are a crucial aspect of good health. Including fermented foods in your regular diet will support digestion and bowel regulation. Kefir is known to improve stool frequency and consistency in people with chronic constipation. Yogurt is also helpful when dealing with constipation that is caused by slow intestinal digestion. Certain foods are easier to digest when fermented. For instance, if you consume sourdough bread instead of non-fermented bread, you will see reduced gas production, less bloating, and less abdominal discomfort.

• Easier Weight Management

Fermented foods help with weight management. Kimchi does this by affecting the genes that are involved in fat cell creation. Yogurt consumption has long been linked to lower BMI and fat percentage in the body. Many nutritionists suggest fermented food for people suffering from obesity or those who are overweight. Fermented foods also tend to be high in dietary fiber, which keeps you feeling full for a longer time. They don't contain too much sugar or cholesterol, and they can be consumed in larger amounts without worrying about gaining weight.

• Better Mental Health

The gut is linked to your mental health, and fermented foods have a beneficial effect on both. When there is an imbalance in the gut microbiome, it affects mental health disorders like depression or anxiety. This is because gut dysbiosis may trigger an inflammatory response. By reducing the levels of such inflammatory microbes, fermented foods support mental health. They also increase the bioavailability of phenolic plant compounds that will modulate neurotransmission. Probiotics have a beneficial effect on the gut-brain axis too.

• Antimicrobial Properties

Fermented foods supply the gut with a better concentration of friendly bacteria and also have antimicrobial effects that reduce undesirable bacteria. These antimicrobial properties help in fighting against pathogenic and opportunistic microbes in the gut. Kefir grains also have antibacterial and antifungal properties that fight against common pathogens like Salmonella typhi, Salmonella enterica, Shigella sonnei, and Candida Albicans. In the Helicobacter pylori infection, kefir can be consumed as an added defense along with antibiotics. The growth of Helicobacter pylori, Campylobacter jejuni, and Salmonella typhimurium is also inhibited by kombucha consumption. Regular consumption of yogurt introduces lactic acid-producing bacteria that have antimicrobial properties in the gut.

• Improves Cognitive Function

Some research suggests that fermented foods may help in improving cognitive function. A study done on mice showed that Lactobacillus pentosus inhibits drug-induced memory impairment. This probiotic is present in kimchi. Another human trial done with functional MRI showed that the consumption of fermented milk products modulates brain activity.

• Boosts the Nutritional Value of Food

Fermentation affects the nutrient content of food. It reduces antinutrients that diminish or stop the absorption of beneficial nutrients in the body. Fermented foods will boost the supply of healthy micronutrients instead. For instance, phytic acid is an antinutrient that reduces mineral absorption. Fermented grain and soybean products will provide microbial phytase that catalyzes phytic acid breakdown and prevent the negative effect on mineral absorption. Sourdough is a fermented food that promotes gluten breakdown and makes it easier to digest for those sensitive to gluten. Beta-galactosidase in kefir reduces the lactose content in it. Fermented foods increase the bioavailability of nutrients like iron, B vitamins, calcium, and zinc by promoting the breakdown of substances that otherwise inhibit their absorption. They also increase dairy product acidity, transforming micronutrients like calcium in these dairy products into bioavailable forms. Specific vitamins like vitamin K2 are synthesized by fermented foods too.

- **Stronger Bones**

For better bone health, fermented milk products are a great option. These products tend to be rich in protein, calcium, vitamin D, phosphorus, and vitamin K2. All of these nutrients are crucial for stronger bones in the body. Studies show that the consumption of kefir helps in bone turnover and better bone mineral density. Fermented milk products may also protect against bone loss that is linked to estrogen deficiency. This may be beneficial for post-menopausal women.

- **Improved Cardiometabolic Health**

Cardiometabolic risk is increased by insulin resistance, hypertension, high triglyceride levels, and many other factors. These factors increase the risk of diabetes type 2, strokes, or cardiovascular disease. Most research suggests that these risk factors may be reduced by increased consumption of fermented foods. Kefir can support healthy blood pressure in a way similar to drugs used for relaxing blood vessels. Adding kimchi as a side dish to each meal for a few months can help lose abdominal fat and reduce body mass index. Insulin resistance is also reduced. Kombucha can help lower blood lipids and blood sugar, thus lowering the risk of fatty liver disease not linked to alcoholism. The risk of blood clots is reduced by consuming natto. Fermented foods help maintain healthy cholesterol levels without having to depend on medication. Tempeh is particularly helpful in this since it provides protein, vitamin B, and fiber that reduce cholesterol build-up in your blood vessels. Studies show that people who consume tempeh regularly have a lower risk of high cholesterol issues.

- Cell Growth Regulation

Some preliminary research suggests that fermented foods help with cell growth regulation. This may help in reducing the risk or spread of cancer in the body. In vitro studies have also shown that kombucha has a toxic effect on cancer cells in the colon. Kombucha consumption may help in preserving the normal epithelial cells in the colon. Certain kimchi-based probiotics can also help in fighting the formation of cancer cells. Consumption of fermented beet juice can inhibit intestinal crypt formation that is considered an early symptom of intestinal cancer.

- Immunity Boost and Reduced Inflammation

Fermented foods have a positive impact on the immune system and can reduce inflammation. Kefir has a probiotic bacterium that has an inhibitory effect on immunoglobulin E production. This molecule takes part in allergic responses. A sugar in kefir called *kefiran* can help prevent allergies since it suppresses mast cell degranulation. Women who consume fermented foods during their pregnancy can help prevent atopic dermatitis in their children.

- Healthier Skin

A healthy gut is reflected in healthy skin. By improving the gut microbiome and reducing inflammation, fermented foods benefit the skin as well. People with acne may benefit from consuming fermented dairy products instead of non-fermented variants. This is because fermentation will reduce insulin-like growth factor 1, responsible for sebum production and inflammation. These foods modulate the gut skin axis and can benefit the skin due to this.

- Protection From Toxins

Promising studies have shown that fermented foods may enhance the ability to detoxify. Lactobacillus is a common species in fermented foods, and it can bind heavy metals and help remove them from the body. Sauerkraut and similar fermented foods contain L. rhamnosus that reduces organophosphate absorption in the gut. The levels of mycotoxins in foods like grains can also be reduced through fermentation. Daily consumption of such fermented foods will help fortify the body against environmental toxins and help cleanse the body.

- ### Increased Energy Levels

For higher quality of life, you need to be healthy and have high levels of energy. If you feel sluggish or lazy, it affects everything that you do. Processed and packaged foods tend to be high in hidden sugars and other additives that leave you feeling tired and lethargic halfway through your day. Fermented foods may help in maintaining higher energy levels. Kombucha is one example of fermented food that is recommended for increasing energy. It has several nutrients like vitamin B that will decrease energy combating factors.

- ### Better Food Absorption

The body needs to be able to absorb important nutrients from the food you consume. However, many factors may affect this. Nutritionists suggest that fermented foods can help in encouraging better food absorption in the body. In particular, foods like tempeh, miso, and kefir will help your body absorb the vitamins and minerals from the other foods you consume. This is why these are regularly consumed as side dishes during meals in Korean and Japanese cuisines.

- ### Preservation of Food

Most of us waste food regularly. We either buy too many vegetables or cook more than we can consume. This food changes when you leave it out on the counter or in your fridge for too long. You will notice that it looks withered or moldy. The food may look like it has melted or gathered colorful mold on its surface. You will also notice a strong unpleasant smell. Once the food is spoiled, you notice these signs and the awful smell. Fermented food smells quite strong as well, but it is not the same as rotten food. Fermentation is a point of balance between the food being spoiled and being preserved.

It allows the good microbes to survive and the bad ones to be removed or killed. If you can carry out the process correctly, you preserve the food and are left with something edible that lasts longer than its original form. Salt often plays a significant role in it since it destroys microbes that usually cause the food to rot or spoil. This allows healthy microbes to thrive in your fermented food, and you can preserve your food for longer.

Points to Remember

• All Fermented Foods Are Not Equal

If you want fermented foods to benefit your body, you need to consume those fermented with natural processes and probiotics. Live cultures are found in kefir, yogurt, kimchi, etc., and so you have a lot from which to choose. The pickled vegetables that you buy from the grocery store may have been pickled with vinegar. Fermented products available in packaged form are often devoid of probiotics since they aren't prepared with the natural fermentation process. To ensure that you are purchasing fermented foods with probiotics, check the label to see if it mentions "naturally fermented." When opening jars of naturally fermented foods, you will usually see some telltale bubbles. These bubbles are a sign that living organisms are present inside. Preparing your own fermented food is the best option, but the next best thing is store-bought if you can find naturally fermented products.

• Moderate Consumption

When it comes to food, everything should be consumed in moderation. You don't have to cut out every food you like to lose weight or get healthy. You shouldn't be overeating something just because you enjoy it, either. Moderate consumption will allow you to enjoy your meals and maintain a healthy body. While we have mentioned numerous benefits of fermented foods, these should be consumed in moderation too. They don't harm your body but should be consumed in reasonable portions. Only then can you expect to benefit from them without worrying about the possible effects of overconsumption.

• Food Safety in Fermentation

Fermentation has been becoming popular again for a good reason. The process allows you to create new flavors from the same old foods and improve your health while you do this. In fact, fermented vegetables are more digestible than in their raw forms. This is because the living bacteria in the fermented vegetables help digest other food present in your digestive tract. People have been fermenting food since ancient times, even without having access to refrigerators or stoves. They managed to do this safely, which says a lot about whether fermented foods are safe for consumption. Most of us eat some form of fermented food every day, but when you are first introduced to the concept and think about fermented foods, you assume it will be pungent and possibly dangerous food. However, your bread, coffee, chocolate, etc., are all fermented foods. Food scientists advocate for the consumption of fermented foods because they are aware of the benefits.

As long as the food is fermented correctly, there is no danger. It is important to know how to ferment the right way to avoid any mishaps. Microbiologist Fred Breidt says that fermented vegetables might be safer to consume than raw vegetables. This is because the lactic acid in fermented foods can find and kill any harmful bacteria. Lactic acid bacteria consume sugars in food and convert them to lactic acid. This lactic acid will then be able to overpower almost any other pathogen nearby. Fermentation methods are easy to follow and similar all across the world. It is hard to mess them up, and although there is a slight possibility of mistakes, it is rare.

Almost all vegetables can be fermented, and cabbage, cucumbers, turnips, radishes, etc., are particularly suited for it. Leafy greens contain high amounts of chlorophyll, and most people don't like the fermented dishes prepared from these. Another thing to keep in mind is that fermentation and pickling overlap but are not the same. For instance, you can pickle cucumbers with or without vinegar and use salty brine instead. Vinegar and other such acids will be produced during fermentation, and this is why they have a vinegary aftertaste. There is still much research on fermentation needed, but most experts agree that the traditional fermentation methods are still as effective as before. People unfamiliar with fermentation are often scared of preparing fermented foods at home because they fear bacteria or assume that the pungent smell means the food has gone bad. But these fears will subside when you realize how common food fermentation is around the world and just how long it has been practiced safely. Sauerkraut has been a constant part of the German diet, especially in winter, since it provides vitamin C and has a high nutritional value. Humans relied on fermentation to preserve food and survive with good health even when food was scarce. The practice of fermenting foods is widespread across the world, and each place has its own fermented food recipes. Some, in particular, have found their way to different places other than their origins and became wildly popular. This book has recipes that will help you safely prepare these fermented dishes without worrying about food safety.

If you are genuinely concerned about food safety, you should know that the basics are the same as preparing any other kind of food. It is better to use vegetables or any other raw ingredient that has been grown organically. If the vegetables you use had come in contact with compost or manure, then they might still have pathogens like Salmonella or E. coli. In such cases, the raw ingredient you use will set you up for failure and harm your health even if you follow the proper fermentation process. Handling the food well and having proper sanitary practices can make a big difference. All produce should be washed thoroughly whether you buy it at a store or grow it in your garden. Wash your hands well before handling food. The surfaces on which you prepare the dish or the utensils you use should also be clean and uncontaminated. For higher quality fermentation, use vegetables that are as fresh as possible. These should help ease your mind on any food safety issues before the preparation of any fermented foods. Handle the food with clean hands or utensils. Don't let it come in contact with any meat or fish that might be contaminated as well. Overall, fermented vegetables have been known to be safer than raw vegetables for consumption. But practicing food safety guidelines helps avoid any possibility of getting sick from fermented food preparation or consumption.

Fermentation alone cannot eliminate every possible health risk associated with food. The correct temperature is crucial. The temperature will determine how much or how little time your food needs to be fermented. For instance, sauerkraut will ferment well in approximately four weeks if the temperature is around 70 degrees. If the temperature goes above 75 degrees, it may get soft. This means that the correct temperature facilitates proper fermentation and allows harmful pathogens to be destroyed while the good microbes thrive.

Salt plays a very important role in the fermentation of foods, so it is essential to measure and add the exact amount of salt mentioned in a tried and tested recipe. Pickling or canning salt is used for fermentation, and these cannot be substituted with kosher salt or table salt. Remember to use salt without added iodine since it may inhibit the fermentation process. The amount of salt appropriate for a dish will depend on what is being fermented.

Certain foods may need nearly 13 percent of their weight in salt, while some might only need around 2.25 percent. The best way to get this right is to follow recipes that are already tested. Someone else's trials and errors will save you time. The salt content will affect the kind and amount of microbial activity taking place while fermenting. It will also prevent your vegetables from getting too soft.

The amount of time you store the fermented food also affects its texture. The vegetables are firmer when they are kept for a shorter time. When you keep fermented food in the fridge, the fermentation rate slows down. This is why you can store fermented foods for a couple of months without their taste or quality being affected. The fermented food should be acidic enough for safe consumption, so check that the pH level is 4.6 or lower.

If the process of fermentation is carried out correctly, this acidic level will be attained easily. Temperature control and following the proper food safety precautions can help avoid any issues like botulism poisoning that bad fermented foods might cause. Using recipes created by food experts or other reputed sources is your best bet. The fermented food recipes in this book are a great way to get started. One of the easiest ways to get started is sauerkraut fermentation.

The basic procedure used for this dish can be used for fermenting many other vegetables too. The fermentation time and salt volume may vary accordingly. For vegetables like carrots that are dense, chop, grate or shred so the lactic acid can easily get inside them. The fermentation is better and safer when the surface area is more. This does not apply to cucumbers since they have a 90 percent volume of water, and the lactic acid bacteria can enter easily.

Another thing to consider when it comes to food safety is mold. A little mold on the surface can happen, and it can be easily removed. If the mold goes down into the solution or food, it increases the risk of disease. Toss out any batch where you notice excess mold formation. It is better to be careful to maintain good health than take undue risks by consuming moldy food.

If you keep all these simple points in mind, you can safely enjoy fermented foods and improve the health of your gut and body.

Chapter Three: Supplies You Will Need

This chapter will cover the supplies you will need to begin fermenting. It will help you understand the importance of using the proper containers for fermenting. It will also act as a guide to buying "starter" cultures or finding them locally.

Although fermenting can be done with minimal supplies, a vast array of tools make the process safer and easier. Below, we've made a list of the most important items and explain how they could be used.

Fermentation Supplies

Fermentation Jars

There are many different kinds of containers that you can use for fermentation. It could be an old pickle jar or even a water-sealed ceramic crock. Any of these will help get the job done. Some make the process easier for you and show better results than others. Getting the suitable jars might make a little bit of a difference after all.

Canning Jars

Canning jars are a great container for you to start with fermentation. They usually come under the labels of Mason, Kilner, Ball, etc., and are readily available. If you are a beginner, the quart-sized jar is perfect for you. It will be just enough for you to make a small batch of kimchi or sauerkraut. You can use these jars to experiment with many fermentation recipes and develop your skills along the way.

When you use different recipes for the same dish in small batches, you can determine which one turns out the best or more to your liking. You can use that recipe to make a bigger batch in the future. These jars are usually relatively cheap, and you can even buy them in bulk. You just need to make sure that the jars you get have wide mouths. Canning jars are handy for many things, so there can never be enough of them in the house.

Clamp Jars

Wire bale clamp jars are another great option for fermentation. They are usually called Fido jars, and many people swear by them. These clamp lids are the perfect way to ensure that your food ferments in an anaerobic environment. An airtight seal is created with the thick gasket and strong wire bale that holds down the lid.

Some people ferment food in these jars with the airlock because they believe that the built-up gases from the fermentation will exert enough pressure on the lid to lift it a bit and allow them to escape through the space between the lid and rubber gasket. If you want to ferment without the airlock, it is better to stick with branded jars made from hardened glass. Instead of cheap knockoffs, buy brands like Fido and Bormioli Rocco. The knockoffs are usually from China and are made of thin glass and low-quality gaskets. These jars can explode if there is too much CO_2 build-up once the fermentation process begins. The hardened glass will help you avoid that.

Choosing between Different Materials for Jars:

- **Glass Containers.** Glass is the most common and best option for fermentation. It does not contain harmful chemicals like BPA and is not easily damaged or scratched like plastic. Glass containers are fairly inexpensive. This makes them a viable option for most people.

- **Ceramic Containers.** Fermentation crocks are usually made of ceramic, and these are an excellent option for fermenting large batches. These ceramic jars can be found at supply stores or local potters.

- **Porcelain Containers.** For fermenting food, you have to get food-grade porcelain jars. Don't use porcelain pieces that are meant for decors like vases or pottery. These are not suitable for food fermentation.

- **Plastic Containers.** Plastic is a cheap option and can technically be used, but it is not recommended for many reasons. Plastic gets damaged, and the scratches in it can harbor harmful bacteria. You need to use food-grade plastic if you choose plastic containers, but even these have undesirable chemicals that should be avoided.

Mixing Bowls

If you want to make large batches of fermented foods, you need large bowls to help you prepare. Most people already have a large mixing bowl in their kitchen, but you need to get one if you don't. A glass or stainless-steel bowl is best, but you can get a plastic one too. It is better not to use copper or aluminum bowls since these metals will react with salt that you might use. You need a wide bowl where you can easily mix your ingredients using your hands. Get a large bowl that is big enough for preparing large and small batches of fermented food.

Fermentation Weights

Another key tool in fermentation is fermentation weights. These weights help keep everything airtight. If you want to pickle vegetables, you will want to use fermentation weights. They will protect your food from yeast and mold growth. There are three kinds of fermentation weights with which you need to be familiar.

Fermentation weights rely on weight to hold the fermented food below the brine. However, these weights are often not heavy enough to do the job, which is a drawback. For instance, when you are fermenting sauerkraut, many air bubbles are created within the jar, which causes the cabbage to expand. The weight is moved up, and the fermenting cabbage will be exposed to air. This prevents fermentation in anaerobic conditions and will prevent you from achieving the best possible results.

Fermentation gates are devices that lock into the neck of a jar and prevent the contents from moving upward. It can be a challenge to pack the jar perfectly when you use a fermentation gate. If you pack it too high, you might get brine overflow. If it is too low, the gate cannot apply force at all and won't be helpful.

Fermentation springs rely on pressure from the coiled spring made of stainless steel to push the ferment under the brine.

Fermentation Lids

Fermentation takes place in an anaerobic environment. This means the process occurs without the presence of air. To allow this, you should ideally use a lid that will seal your jar in a way that will reduce the chance of any yeast or mold growing on the surface. You can simply use the lids that usually come with the canning jars you purchase. You can also get special fermentation lids that have a one-way valve, airlock, or water-sealed moat. There are many different kinds of fermentation lids from which you can choose.

Fermentation Lids with No Airlock

Plastic storage caps are a better option than the metal lids on canning jars. Plastic lids don't corrode like metal ones and do a much better job. A lid with a seal will work better to keep the air out from your ferment. Lids without airlocks should not be screwed on too tightly because the active fermentation stage causes a build-up of gases and may cause the jar to explode. Silicone gaskets or lids with silicone gaskets can be used to make the jar airtight and leakproof.

Fermentation Lids with Airlocks

Lids with an airlock may allow gases to escape but will prevent any new air from entering the jar. Many fermenting experts say that this allows a better ferment with higher levels of good bacteria. You can get these lids in stainless steel, plastic, or silicone for your jars. Some lids even have an extractor pump that will allow you to suction out air from the jar. This should be done before the fermented product is refrigerated or right after the first week of fermentation.

Cloth Covers

Some people choose to use cloth covers for fermenting certain foods. If you have a small container, you can use a coffee filter to cover the top and secure it with a canning lid ring or just a tight rubber band. This will keep out any pests and will let fermentation gases escape. For jars that are a little bigger, you can use a tight weave dishcloth or some butter muslin.

Secure this around the mouth of the jar with a rubber band. The advantage of using cloth covers is that you can easily taste or sneak a peek at the fermenting food whenever you want. The disadvantage is that the surface of the fermented food will likely form some mold or kahm yeast. Although this surface formation can be removed easily and is harmless, it is better to avoid this risk and use other lids. Cheesecloth is one of the best options to use as a cloth lid. It is a breathable fabric that will keep contaminants out of your jars.

Digital Scale

Another important fermentation tool is a digital scale. Using the correct amounts of each ingredient for your fermentation recipe can make a huge difference in how it turns out. If you are making kimchi or sauerkraut, you need to measure out the right amount of salt required for fermentation. Using the correct amount of salt will ensure that the lactobacilli can do their job well. This is important for preserving the ferment safely.

When you buy a digital scale, you need to check for a few things. See if the display is clearly visible when you place a large bowl on the scale. The scale should also be capable of weighing at least ten pounds or more if you make large batches. It will also be helpful if you can get a scale that can be programmed not to shut off automatically. There are all kinds of scales available these days, and you can have your pick. Try to get one with high-precision sensors and multiple weighing modes to make your job easier.

Water Sealed Fermentation Crocks

Quart jars are for beginners or smaller portions. Once you have enough experience, you can move on to a large crock specifically meant for fermenting larger quantities of food. Specialty crocks have a more stable environment that allows better fermentation. They come with water-sealed lids that enable fermentation gases to escape without allowing air to enter. This helps in maintaining an environment ideal for anaerobic fermentation. A 5-liter crock is usually enough for a small family. If you want to make kimchi or sauerkraut, this jar would easily pack ten pounds of cabbage. It is also not too big and can be picked up easily. A crock that is any bigger would be too heavy to move around and difficult to clean in the sink as well.

Mineral-Rich Fermentation Salt

For sauerkraut, the cabbage is fermented in brine, which is prepared with salt. The salt pulls out water from the cabbage and other vegetables, creating an environment where gut-friendly bacteria grow and proliferate. The harmful bacteria will die in this brine. Using mineral-rich salts that retain their natural mineral profile is often a better choice. Fermentation makes the minerals bioavailable, and this is why your sauerkraut will be more nutritious.

Himalayan pink salt is a great option that is mined from deposits in the Himalayan Mountains. It contains high amounts of trace minerals, and the pink color is due to the iron oxide that is naturally present in this salt. This pink salt is dug from deep within the mountains, crystallized nearly 200 million years ago. It is not affected by any impurities and pollution from the modern world.

Mandolin

Mandolins are stainless steel or plastic devices that are used for slicing fruits and vegetables. They have interchangeable blades depending on the kind of slicing you want to do. Blades made of surgical steel are the sharpest and best option for preparing your vegetables. Getting consistent texture and evenly sliced pieces will make your sauerkraut taste even better. When you have uneven pieces with some thick and others thin, the sauerkraut does not turn out the way it should. Making thread cuts for sauerkraut is recommended since it exposes more of the cabbage cells, releasing more lactic acid bacteria.

As long as you keep the mandolin clean, you won't have to replace or sharpen the blade very often. Mandolins are also easier to clean than most food processors.

Redmond Real Salt

In Central Utah, there are ancient sea beds from which Real Salt is mined. You can buy this from most grocery stores or specialty health food stores. Unlike other salts, it is subtly sweet and has high amounts of trace minerals. Look for the unprocessed and unrefined kind with no additives.

Safety Gloves

You might want to get right into it with your hands, but safety gloves might be a better option. Especially when you want to slice vegetables or fruits with tools like the mandolin, it is better to be safe than sorry. Safety gloves will protect your hands and are also comfortable enough to use while mixing. You can use your bare hands through most of the fermentation preparation process but use gloves when dealing with sharp tools or reactive ingredients.

Kraut Pounder, Funnels

Not everyone has the hand strength required to crush the cabbage leaves thoroughly. This is where the kraut pounder comes in. Kraut pounders help you mix and pound your vegetables quickly in a large bowl, so the natural juices are released. This tool is also helpful for pressing down vegetables into a jar when the mouth isn't too wide. When your hand doesn't fit into the jar, the pounder is the easier alternative.

You can use it to pack fermented foods into small jars. This tool isn't a complete necessity since you can just use a large spoon, meat pounder, or rolling pin for the same purpose. It's always nice to have separate tools for your fermentation recipes. Getting a wide-mouth funnel will also make the packing part a little easier. This tool is helpful if you intend to use a kraut pounder but will only get in the way when you use your hands to stuff the jars.

pH scale

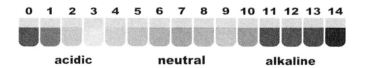

0 1 2 3 4 5 6 7 8 9 10 11 12 13 14

acidic   **neutral**   **alkaline**

It can sometimes be hard for beginners to tell if they have a good ferment or just spoiled food. The pungent smell is not always a good indicator. In such cases, pH strips can be used to see if the ferment is safe for consumption. Buy pH strips that are in the lower range between 0.0 and 6.0. Just ladle out a little bit of your brine or any other fermented solution and dip a pH strip into it. The ferment is safe to eat if the pH level is 4.0 or lower. These strips are easy to read and can be pretty useful.

Thermometers

Fermentation takes place in a specific ideal temperature range. You have to check if the temperature is just right or if you have to make some adjustments to the duration of fermentation. The temperature can determine whether you need to let it ferment for a shorter or longer time. This is where a thermometer may be useful. Get a room thermometer that you can use for monitoring the humidity and temperature.

Auto Siphon

Auto siphons will allow you to transfer liquid from one vessel to another in a sanitary way. This tool will come in handy when transferring your fermented food from a large vessel to smaller containers. It is useful when bottling something like kombucha, does not disrupt the liquid, and you don't risk contaminating it.

Specialty Spices

Depending on what fermented dish you want to prepare, you will need to buy some ingredients. For certain dishes like kimchi, you need specialty spices. Korean red pepper powder or Gochugaru is one spice that you should purchase in bulk and keep. It adds an authentic flavor and color to kimchi and can even be used in sauerkraut. These days it is easy to buy spices online or in Asian food stores. Buy a lot so you can use it whenever you run out of kimchi. This spice is made from coarsely ground red pepper, and the texture is a mix of powder and flakes.

The flavor is more complex than your regular red pepper flakes, and it adds beautiful color to the dish. Sun-dried chili peppers will give you the best Gochugaru. You can extend the shelf life of this spice by storing it in the freezer. The amount of gochugaru you use will determine the heat in the dish.

Bottle brush

When you are done with a batch of fermented wine, kombucha, etc., you need to clean the bottles out. Clean jars or bottles are a must when you want to ferment a new batch of food. If not, these can harbor foreign bacteria that will spoil the food and harm your gut. Get a brush with bristles that will clean the necks and corners of your containers thoroughly. Scrub them out and wash them thoroughly to prepare for the subsequent fermentation batch.

Fish Sauce

Yet another ingredient that is a must for some fermented Asian dishes is fish sauce. It is especially important for preparing kimchi. Don't worry about getting a fishy taste or smell in the dish because it goes away once the fermentation happens. Instead, it will add a richness that will make your kimchi more authentic. Fish sauce will also be useful in cooking other Asian dishes at home, so you can get a bigger bottle and store it in the fridge.

Refractometer

A refractometer with Auto Thermal Compensation (ATC) is not essential, and not everyone uses one, but if you are serious about fermenting foods, this might be useful. This tool will help you identify components and levels of ingredients in your fermentation solutions. This will allow you to calculate the alcohol percentage of a beverage. For instance, you can read sugar levels when you make drinks like tepache, a fermented drink made from pineapple. It will also be helpful when making kombucha, beer, wine, etc.

Saniclean

When it comes to food, keeping things clean and hygienic is very important. This is more so when fermenting foods since the kitchen is always exposed to bacteria and yeast. The counter on which you ferment should be extremely clean. Saniclean is one of the best food-safe and affordable disinfectants out there. Saniclean is in line with industry standards, and you can even wash your utensils with a diluted solution. This will ensure that all your counters and utensils are completely clean and safe for storing or fermenting foods.

Starter Cultures

Now let's talk a little more about starter cultures. You have to know when you need to use starters, when you don't and why whey is unnecessary.

Fungi and bacteria play a crucial role in the process of fermentation. Fungi usually produce alcohol, while bacteria produce acids. Certain foods require their use separately, but with others, you will need a mixture of both. Fungi are used for preparing bread, cheese, and wine, while bacteria are involved in yogurt or sauerkraut preparation.

When lactic acid-producing bacteria metabolize sugars in food and convert them to lactic acid, it is called Lacto fermentation. The bacteria are isolated in milk first, and this is why they are called lactic acid-forming bacteria. Lactobacillus is found in many places and not just exclusively present in milk or other dairy products.

Lacto fermentation is used for preparing many foods like sauerkraut, kefir, yogurt, and beet kvass. Unlike ethanol fermentation, alcohol is not created with Lacto fermentation. Lactic acid bacteria are microbes that primarily consume carbohydrates that are naturally found in cucumber. This is how you prepare sour pickles.

Many beginners assume that the fermentation process to make foods like sauerkraut will require dairy products like whey. This is just a myth, and you don't need whey at all. Whey was popularly used before for preparing fermented vegetables, but this method is not as popular now. The bacteria that cause lactic acid fermentation are present everywhere, from your skin to your food and even on your countertops. This is why it is not necessary to inoculate foods with starters like whey. In fact, fermented foods will turn out even better without them.

Starters Are Not Required for Most Fermented Foods

Most fermented vegetable recipes don't require the use of starter culture and were traditionally prepared without one. Salting the vegetables will do the same job, and you can just pack them into your fermentation containers for the native bacteria to do their job. This will allow the vegetables to naturally sour and be preserved without needing any starter. You can store them for a long time with salt once they are fermented. Traditionally, vegetables were fermented without any starter culture, and this method is called wild fermentation. It involves using wild strains of bacteria for fermentation and not domesticated strains found in starter cultures.

Some fermented preparations require a starter culture, while others do not. Fermented vegetables like kimchi, sauerkraut, sour pickles, sauerruben, etc., do not need starter cultures. You also don't need them for preserving limes, lemons, or bonny clabber.

Certain foods require a starter to ensure that they can be safely consumed and have consistent texture and flavor results. Sourdough bread is one example that requires a starter. You can make this starter with wild fermentation or get a starter from another baker. A mother culture has to be used if you want Jun tea or Kombucha to be brewed properly. Water kefir grains are needed for preparing water kefir. Yogurt preparation requires a starter culture as well. Homemade sodas like probiotic lemonade and root beer depend on starter cultures.

For making kombucha, you need to use sweetened black tea. If this tea is left in a container on some shelf, it won't turn sour on its own and is likely to mold. Once you add a mother culture to the tea, the yeast and bacterial strains from the culture will consume the sugar in the tea and turn it into acids. This will give the kombucha a pleasantly tart flavor and added B vitamins.

If you leave raw milk in its own container, it will turn sour, and a bonny clabber will be formed. This is a wild-fermented product that has an inconsistent flavor and texture in each batch. If you want consistent results from your raw milk, use a yogurt starter culture. This will allow you to make batches of Bulgarian-style yogurt that is sweet and tart or villi yogurt that is ropy and viscous. Using a starter gives you the ability to make consistent batches of fermented food.

Then there are fermented foods that don't require a starter but benefit from the use of starter culture. This means that you get better results by using the starter rather than by depending on wild fermentation. These are usually foods that only ferment for a short time, like high sugar fruits or condiments.

Adding a starter culture to foods fermenting for short durations kickstarts the process and gives you reliable results. If you want to make homemade fermented condiments like mustard or ketchup, a few days of fermentation will give you maximum flavor. It is challenging to keep these submerged in a brine solution since they are pastes. They remain exposed to oxygen and tend to get contaminated by mold. When the starter culture is inoculated, it shortens the time needed and reduces the chances of mold contamination.

Fruits with high amounts of sugar usually turn alcoholic if they are fermented for a long time. If you don't want an alcoholic fermentation and just want to prepare a relish, condiment, or sauce, the fermentation time needs to be shorter. This can be achieved by introducing a starter culture. It will speed up the process and give you a rich fermented product with many beneficial bacteria without being alcoholic. Certain fermented foods like beet kvass have been traditionally prepared using starter cultures. The use of a starter is a choice and not a necessity. Following the traditional way of using a starter, in this case, will give you better results.

Which Starter Do You Use?

Some popular fermentation guides recommend the use of whey in preparing most fermented foods. This is why beginners tend to use this as a starter for all their fermented food recipes. They use whey drawn from clabbering raw milk or making yogurt as a starter. This is a good option since it is abundant and inexpensive. You can use most liquids rich in beneficial bacteria as a starter culture. You can also purchase a store-bought packet of starter culture if you want.

If you want to consume a particular strain of bacteria for its benefits, you need to look for a starter culture that contains those strains.

The following are some starter cultures you can try using:
- Kombucha or Jun tea
- Brine from fermenting vegetables like sauerkraut juice
- Water kefir
- Commercial packaged starter culture
- Probiotic supplements
- The whey is obtained by straining kefir, yogurt, or clabbered raw milk.

Fermented foods usually don't need a starter, but using the right equipment can make all the difference in the end. You can try a starter for the foods that call for it in the recipe. These starter cultures are easy to get, but you should only use them for fermented foods that really need them.

Once you learn the basics of fermentation, it gets easy to experiment and to prepare new fermented dishes. You can virtually ferment any fruit or vegetable you like and make sodas from juices or teas. Try the recipes in this book and learn how to make your favorite fermented foods to improve your overall health.

Chapter Four: How to Make Kombucha

Kombucha is an incredibly healthy fermented drink that can be dated back, through China, Tibet, and Japan, at least a couple of thousand years. However, we cannot determine its exact origin. Made from sweetened tea, kombucha grew fast in popularity, spreading through Russia, the USA, and Europe.

Most standard fizzy drinks you buy these days are made from sugar, artificial flavoring, and carbonated water. Kombucha differs in that it is *alive* – the natural fermentation process causes the carbonation, and its flavors are also natural. Seriously, take a sip of a shop-bought fizzy drink and then a sip of kombucha – the difference is amazing, especially when you make your own kombucha.

Making kombucha is a fantastic project – you get to dabble in microbiology and produce whatever flavor you want, using ingredients of your choice. The only limit is here is your imagination.

What Is Scoby?

Making kombucha requires scoby, an acronym for Symbiotic Culture of Bacteria and Yeast. Scoby is shaped like a disk, a necessary culture to help the fermentation process convert the sweet tea into the kombucha. Typically, scoby floats on the top of the batch, but don't panic if yours should sink! It is still active and doing its job.

Where do you get this scoby? If you've got friends already making kombucha, the easiest way is to ask if you can have some scoby. If not, you can purchase it online or make your own. I've provided a step-by-step guide on making your own scoby below – try it; it's all part of the process.

If you purchase your scoby or get it from a friend, it will have liquid with it, which goes into your first batch. You must make sure this liquid goes in because it has large amounts of yeast and bacteria and a great deal of acid that creates the proper environment for subsequent batches.

Every scoby is different and is a result of the environment in which it was created. It contains many different yeasts that go far beyond your standard Saccharomyces cerevisiae – a beer and bread fermenter. These yeasts include Brettanomyces bruxellensis and

Schizosaccharomyces pombe (also called "fission yeast), along with lots of bacteria species responsible for limiting alcohol content and increasing acidity.

Equipment

You don't need to purchase expensive equipment to make kombucha. The chances are you already have some of what you need. The important thing is to use glass jars or ceramic if its glaze is food-grade, but *not metal or plastic*. Wide-mouthed jars are much better as the larger surface area ensures a faster fermentation process.

Important Considerations

• Use de-chlorinated water because chlorine negatively affects the microbes we want to grow. Tap water is chlorinated, and a standard water filter will not receive the chlorine either. Boil and cool the water or leave it in a bowl overnight so the chlorine dissipates.

• Use black tea as it has all the nutrients required by the scoby. However, you may prefer a mixture of green and black or white and black tea; it's entirely up to you. Use loose tea or tea bags and avoid using tea like Earl Gray, which has added oils. You can also use plant-based tea, such as chamomile, raspberry leaf, nettle, rooibos, etc. However, try to make at least a quarter of the tea black in every batch or couple of batches. Lastly, use organic tea where you can.

• Try to use ordinary cane sugar. You can use less refined sugars, but they will change the flavor. You cannot omit the sugar because it feeds the bacteria and yeast to reproduce, creates new scobies, and processes the tea into carbonation, vitamins, and acids. Once fermentation is complete, most of the remaining sugar has been broken down into glucose and fructose. The bacteria transform it into healthy acids, and then the enzymes get to work, breaking the sugars down further. If you don't use enough sugar, your scoby will starve. Do not use honey as it contains different bacteria cells and yeasts, and do not use sugar substitutes or artificial sugars, as they won't feed the yeast or bacteria.

• When you begin your second or subsequent batches of kombucha, make sure you use starter liquid taken from the previous batch – this should be 10% of the new batch and is used to lower the tea's pH. Typically, kombucha has a pH of 3.5 to 2.5, whereas tap water is 7. Lower pH numbers indicate acidity, but you don't have to measure it – you'll taste it. The starter liquid is essential to protect the tea from kahm yeast, mold, or other harmful microorganisms.

All the equipment should be clean and dry.

• 1 to 2 glass jars (2-quart glass jar or 2 one-quart glass jars) or bigger if required, with airtight lids
• Stock pot
• Glass bottles or jars with plastic lid for storage
• Tightly woven cloth or lint-free cloth
• Funnel
• Strainer
• Rubber band
• Container to keep Scoby (symbiotic culture of bacteria and yeast) which is used for fermentation
• Kombucha and Scoby

Makes: 6 cups

Preparation time: 10 minutes

Fermenting time: 2-4 weeks

Ingredients:

For Scoby:

- 2 cups water
- 4 tablespoons granulated or raw sugar
- 2 tablespoons unflavored loose leaf black tea or 4 black tea bags
- 2 bottles (16 ounces each) unflavored, raw, unpasteurized, good quality kombucha with sediment

For Kombucha:

- 6 cups water
- 6 tablespoons granulated or raw sugar
- 4 tablespoons loose-leaf black tea leaves or 8 black tea bags
- 1 cup kombucha starter tea
- 1 scoby for every jar (¼ to ½ inch thick)

Directions:

To Make Scoby:

1. Boil water in a stockpot. Turn off the heat. Drop the tea bags or tea leaves into the water. Let it brew for 5 to 10 minutes. Remove the tea bags or strain the tea into a jar. Add sugar and stir until sugar dissolves completely.

2. Set aside to cool completely. Add kombucha with the sediment and mix well.

3. Keep the jar covered with cloth and tighten with a rubber band. Place it in an area without direct sunlight, at a temperature between 75° and 80°.

4. Slowly, in a few days, scoby will start forming on top of the liquid. You may find string-like things or some dots of mass. It will slowly grow into one big mass. This can take anywhere between 2 to 4 weeks until the scoby is at least ¼ inch thick.

5. The scoby can be used now.

6. The liquid remaining in the jar is the starter tea you can use to make kombucha.

To Make Kombucha:

1.   Boil water in a stockpot. Turn off the heat. Drop the tea bags or tea leaves into the water. Let it brew for 5 to 10 minutes. Remove the tea bags or strain the tea into a jar. Add sugar and stir until sugar dissolves completely.

2.   Set aside to cool completely. Add kombucha with the sediment and mix well.

For the First Fermentation:

1.Place scoby in the jar, making sure your hands are clean before adding scoby.

2.Keep the jar covered with cloth and fasten with a rubber band. Place it in an area without direct sunlight, at a temperature between 75° and 80°.

3.Let it ferment for 3 – 4 days. Start tasting it after 3 to 4 days. Keep an eye out for the scoby. New scoby will begin to form on the surface of the kombucha. It should be cream-colored. It generally tends to form on top of the old scoby.

4.If you think it is not good enough, ferment it for longer, around 7 to 10 days. When you find the taste pleasant, your kombucha is ready. It should have a sweet, though pungent (strong).

5.When the desired taste is achieved, you need to start with the second fermentation.

For the Second Fermentation (Carbonation):

1. Clean your hands and take out the scoby from the jar. Keep the scoby in a clean container. If you are going to brew more kombucha soon (in a couple of days), place the scoby at a temperature between 75° and 80°.

2. If you are going to brew after 2 to 3 weeks, place it in a glass jar or airtight container Ziploc bag in the fridge. Pour some of the kombucha so it's immersed in the kombucha. Place one scoby per jar. Place it in the fridge. Do not keep it for longer than three months.

3. Stir the prepared kombucha and retain about a cup of kombucha to make a new batch of kombucha.

4. Pour the remaining kombucha into storage bottles using the funnel. Do not fill right up to the top. Leave neck space of at least 2 inches.

5. The flavorings can be added now (below are some flavoring options, but you can make your own flavorings). For this much quantity of kombucha, use about ¼ to ½ cup fresh fruit juice or fresh fruit puree, or some chopped fruit. You can also add 2 – 4 tablespoons of fresh herbs. If you are using chopped fruit, make sure the fruits are immersed in water as they may end up getting moldy if they float on top. The choice is ultimately yours to use chopped fruit, puree, or juice. You can add any other spices or flavorings of your choice. After adding flavorings, stir well.

6. Fasten the lid and keep it in a place with no direct sunlight for about 2 to 3 days. You can ferment it for longer if desired. Make sure to open the bottle once daily, to remove extra carbonation.

7. When you get the desired taste, place the bottles in the fridge until use. Below are some flavor options.

Ideas for Flavored Kombucha

Now for the flavoring. Your options are endless, and you can use all different vegetables, fruits, and herbs, frozen, fresh, dried, or even juiced. How much you use depends on whether you want a subtle flavor or something more intense, but 5 to 10% is normally sufficient if using fresh fruit. That equates to 2 to 3 tablespoons per liter.

The easiest way to do it is to cut your fruit, veg or herbs into small chunks and add them to an empty bottle. Then fill the bottle with kombucha, but be sure to leave four fingers of space at the top because carbon dioxide will build up - if you don't leave the space, the whole lot will explode. Leave it at room temperature for 24 hours to allow the yeast to turn some of the sugars into carbon dioxide and then place it in the refrigerator. This will stop the entire process and prevent the bacteria from creating even more acid.

Some flavor ideas:

You can use pretty much any fruit you like, either on its own or a few combined.

- **Berries** - a mixture of berries, such as blackberries, strawberries, and blueberries,

- **Stone fruits** - plums, peaches, and cherries. These will give your kombucha a stunning flavor and beautiful color.

- **Citrus fruits** – use chunks of fruit, the zest, or the juice. If you use the zest, make sure the fruit has not been waxed.

- **Exotic fruit** – such as goji berries, cranberries, figs, and dates. Do not use raisins or any oil-soaked fruit, or apricots, and any other fruit containing sulfur dioxide, as this can make your kombucha taste of rotten eggs.

- **Frozen fruit** –the ice crystals created during the freezing process break the fruit's cell structure down, which means the kombucha benefits from more flavor and color. However, you can also use puree or juice.

- **Herbs** – lemon balm, mint, lavender, and other herbs work well on their own or with fruit, such as strawberries paired with thyme, mint, and apple, raspberries with basil, and so on.

- **Spices** – mild spices can be used alone or blended or with a fruit pairing. You can use burdock, turmeric, allspice, cloves, coriander, star anise, peppercorn, cinnamon, cardamom, licorice, or juniper, to name a few. Hot spices you can use include ginger, jalapeno, or cayenne.

- **Vegetables** – carrot, cucumber, and beetroot provide lovely flavors, while garlic provides a kick and pairs well with lemon. You can even use mushrooms.
- **Other** – you can try cacao powder, brewed coffee, maca powder, tamarind, coconut water, rose petals, rosehips, and so on.

Here are some recipes you can try out:

(for about 6 cups prepared kombucha)

You can puree, juice, or finely chop fruits and add them to the bottles or jars

Watermelon

Ingredients:

- 6 – 8 small watermelon cubes, deseeded

Lime and Lemon

Ingredients:

- 3 – 4 teaspoons lime juice
- 3 – 4 tablespoons lemon juice
- 2 thin ginger slices
- 2 thin lemon slices

Blueberry Ginger

Ingredients:

- 6 – 7 peeled, thinly sliced ginger, pricked with a fork
- A handful of blueberries, pricked with a fork

Blackberry Mango

Ingredients:

- 4 – 5 small mango cubes (about ½ inch cubes)
- A small handful of blackberries, pricked with a fork

Lemon Ginger & Honey

Ingredients:

- 4 – 5 tablespoons lemon juice
- 1 tablespoon honey
- 3-inch piece of ginger, peeled and grated

Chapter Five: How to Make Sourdough Bread

Sourdough bread has recently risen in popularity – if you'll pardon the pun – and many think it is a far tastier bread than standard, not to mention healthier. Some even go so far as to say it is much easier to digest and won't send your blood sugar spiking. But, what is it, and how is it so different from conventional bread?

Sourdough is one of the most ancient forms of grain fermentation, believed to have begun around 1500 BC in Egypt and remaining as the primary method of leavening bread until a few centuries ago, when baker's yeast came into the picture.

Leavened bread rises as a result of gas produced while the grain is fermenting. These days, commercial baker's yeast is used in most leavened bread, but traditional methods still use two things found naturally in flour – lactic acid and wild yeast.

Wild yeast resists acid better than baker's yeast, and this is why it works well with the bacteria producing the lactic acid to help the bread dough rise. You will also find lactic acid in kefir, sauerkraut, yogurt, kimchi, and pickles, all the best-fermented foods on the planet.

Sourdough bread requires a "starter," a mixture of lactic acid bacteria, wild yeast, water, and flour. This mixture ferments the sugars present in the dough, which helps it rise and gives it its unique taste. Also, sourdough bread takes longer to ferment and rise than conventional bread, giving it a specific texture.

You can buy sourdough bread in many stores these days, but the traditional methods are not used to make it, and they are nowhere near as healthy as what you make at home. So don't do things the quick way – make your own; I promise you won't regret it.

Let's look at how the starter and sourdough bread are made.

Weigh all the ingredients on a weighing scale, including the water. The containers used should be made of glass or plastic (make sure it is not made of any metals) and should be clean and dry.

Equipment Required:

There are different methods of baking, so all these may not be needed. Some of these items are used in each recipe.

- Oven
- Dutch oven
- Mixing bowl
- Glass jar
- Kitchen towels
- Rubber bands
- Roasting pan

- Baking stone
- Bench scraper

Sourdough Starter

It takes a minimum of five days to make the starter, depending on the temperature of your kitchen. It can take up to seven days. So you need to start making the starter at least 5 – 7 days before making the bread. If it's cold out, it will take around seven days. If it's warm out, it will take about five days.

Feeding Your Starter

Everyone who bakes sourdough bread will find their own method of feeding their starter, but this is the basic method.

- Pour around half the culture off, and then add equal weights of water and flour to the remaining starter.

- Whisk thoroughly with a fork until there are no more lumps

- Leave it at room temperature or somewhere warm, at about 75 to 80°F, until it begins bubbling and becomes active.

You will know it is ready when it bubbles and has expanded to double its size. This may be 2 to 12 hours, depending on the temperature – warmer temperatures are better – and also depends on your starter's condition. The most important thing is to be patient.

If you are still not sure your starter is ready, drop a teaspoon of it into water. If it floats, it's ready. If it sinks, it needs feeding again.

Here's how to make it.

Makes: About 1 ¼ cups of starter

Ingredients:

For the first day:

- 1.4 ounces whole-wheat flour or rye flour
- 1.4 ounces all-purpose flour

- 1.4 ounces water

For each following day:

- 1.4 ounces whole-wheat flour or rye flour
- 1.4 ounces all-purpose flour
- 1.4 ounces water

Directions:

First day:

1. Step 1: Weigh the ingredients for the first day and add them into a glass jar. If you want to make a rye sourdough starter, use rye flour instead of whole-wheat flour. Stir constantly for a few minutes until well combined. The mixture will be thick and sticky.

2. Step 2: Cover the container loosely with a plastic wrap or clean kitchen towel. If you are using a kitchen towel, put a rubber band around the container to keep it tight. Place at constant room temperature at about 75° F to 78° F. You can keep it on top of your fridge. Make sure the jar isn't exposed to direct sunlight.

Second Day:

1. Step 3: Make sure you feed the starter around the same time every day.

2. Step 4: After 24 hours, a few bubbles may be visible at some places on the dough, and it shows the presence of wild yeast in the starter. You should be able to get a fresh, mild, and sweet smell. If the bubbles are not visible, that is okay. It may be because of the temperature. It takes longer in cold weather.

3. Step 5: You have to activate the starter (also called feeding the starter): For this, retain about 1.4 ounces (3 tablespoons) of the starter in the container and discard the rest.

4. Step 6: Weigh the other ingredients for each following day, i.e., whole-wheat flour, water, and all-purpose flour. Add the weighed ingredients into the container with the starter and stir

until well combined. Keep the jar covered loosely with plastic wrap or a kitchen towel.

Third Day:

1. More bubbles should be visible all over the starter mixture.

2. Try stirring the starter, you can hear tiny bubbles popping, and the batter will be thick. The batter will smell sour and stale. Repeat steps 5 – 6.

Fourth Day:

1. Many more bubbles should be visible all over the starter mixture.

2. When you stir the starter, the batter will be looser to touch, and the smell will be more pungent and sourer than day 3.

Repeat steps 5 – 6.

Fifth Day:

1. The starter will be filled with bubbles, and it will look frothy. The dough should be nearly twice the size of the previous day.

2. The dough will be looser to touch compared to the previous day. Repeat steps 5 – 6.

Sixth Day:

1. The starter is now ripe and can be used to make sourdough bread.

2. To check for ripeness, drop a tablespoon of the starter in a bowl of lukewarm water. If the starter floats, it is ripe and can be used to make sourdough bread. If it does not float, you need to feed the starter again. Repeat steps 5 – 6.

To Maintain the Starter:

1. If you are not making the sourdough bread on the 6th day and you want to make it in the next 2 – 3 days, you need to maintain the starter. Repeat steps 5 – 6 daily until you make the sourdough bread.

2. If you want to use the starter after 2 - 3 weeks, store the jar in the fridge (after covering with cling wrap loosely) and feed the starter once in 6 - 7 days (Repeat steps 5 - 6).

To Dry the Starter:

If you want to store the starter for a longer time, you need to dry the starter:

1. Spread the starter on a Silpat and allow it to dry naturally.

2. After it dries, crumble into smaller pieces.

3. Transfer into an airtight container. It can last for months. Place it at room temperature in a dry area.

To Activate the Dry Starter:

1.   Mix dry starter and some water in a bowl. Cover it loosely and set it aside for 6 - 12 hours.

2.   Start feeding the starter daily (Repeat steps 5 - 6) until the starter is ripe.

Note: If you live in a warm place, you have to feed the starter twice a day, every 12 hours. Also, instead of discarding the starter, you can use it for other recipes like pancakes, etc.

Sourdough Bread

Ingredients:

- 1 cup + 1 tbsp. water
- ¾ cup bubbly, active sourdough starter
- 25 g olive oil
- 2 ¼ cups bread flour
- ½ tbsp. fine sea salt

Directions:

1. Whisk the water, starter, and olive oil in a bowl using a fork.

2. Add the flour and salt and use your hands to squish it together until the flour has been completely absorbed. You should have a dry, shaggy, rough dough.

3. Cover it with plastic wrap, a damp kitchen town, or wax wrap, and leave it to autolyze (rest) for about half an hour.

4. Work the dough into a rough ball in the bowl.

5. Cover it and leave it at room temperature, around 68 to 70°F, and leave it to rise. It will take up to 12 hours and is ready when it is twice the size and not dense anymore. It will take three to four hours in warmer temperatures, while it will take 10 to 12 hours in colder temperatures. However, *don't clock-watch* - your dough is ready when it has properly risen.

6. About half an hour into the rising session, you can stretch and fold the dough if you want. This process gives it more strength, height, and better structure – but only do it if you want to.

7. Once the dough has risen, tip it onto a lightly floured cutting board.

8. Divide it in half using a sharp knife or dough cutter if you are making two loaves, or leave it as is if you only want one.

9. Fold the dough into the center, turn it slightly and fold the next bit over. Repeat for an entire circle.

10. Once your dough is shaped, it must be left to rise again, and this is done in the Dutch oven you will cook the bread in.

11. Line the Dutch oven pot with non-stick parchment paper or a generous cornmeal coating and place the dough in it. Alternatively, use an 8-inch bowl or a proofing basket lined with cloth - that way, the dough is contained and holds the shape.

12. This time, we are only leaving for between 30 minutes and an hour - when it is puffy and not dense, it is ready - don't wait for it to double in size (it won't.)

13. In the last half of the second rise, preheat the oven to 450°F

14. Once the second rise is done, slash a 2 to 3 inch cut along the center of the dough using a paring knife or a small, serrated knife - this will let the steam out of the bread and let the dough expand while baking.

15. Time to bake - we use Dutch ovens because they keep the moisture and heat trapped in, providing the artisan style we've come to know and love. Steam also plays an important role in opening the bread up while baking, and Dutch ovens control this very well. That said, you can use any pot, so long as it is oven safe up to 450°F, including the handles and lid.

16. Place the lid on the pot and turn the temperature down to 400°F. Bake the bread in the center of the oven for about 20 minutes.

17. Remove the lid, and your bread should look shiny and pale

18. Leaving the bread uncovered, bake for about 40 minutes or until it is a deep gold-brown color. The internal temperature should be 205 to 210°F. If you want a crisp crust, crack the over door open slightly during the final 10 minutes of cooking time or turn the bread out and bake it on the wire rack.

19. Turn the bread out onto a wire rack and leave it for at least one hour or until cool before you slice it. *Patience is required here* - if you cut it too soon, it will be gummy.

Blueberry Sourdough Muffins

Makes: 24

Ingredients:

- 2 cups unbleached all-purpose flour
- 1 ½ teaspoons salt
- 3 teaspoons ground cinnamon
- 2 cups whole-grain yellow cornmeal
- 2 teaspoons baking soda
- 1 cup maple syrup or molasses or honey
- Coarse sugar to sprinkle
- 2 cups sourdough starter, ripe or discard
- 2 large eggs
- ½ cup milk
- ½ cup melted butter or vegetable oil
- 4 cups blueberries, fresh or frozen

Directions:

1. As you preheat your oven to 425°F, take two muffin pans, 12 counts each, and spray cooking spray into the cups. Place disposable liners in the cups as well.

2. Combine flour, salt, cinnamon, cornmeal, and baking soda in a bowl.

3. Place starter, eggs, maple syrup, butter, and milk in another bowl and beat with an electric hand mixer until well combined.

4. Pour the egg mixture into the bowl of the flour mixture and beat until just combined, making sure not to overbeat.

5. Add blueberries and fold gently. Do not thaw the blueberries if you are using frozen blueberries.

6. Pour the batter into the muffin cups. Fill up to 2/3.

7. Sprinkle coarse sugar on top.

8. Put the muffin pans in the oven for baking and bake for 25 minutes. To check if the muffins are done, insert a toothpick in the center of a muffin and pull it out. If you find that some particles are stuck on it, then you need to bake for another 5 - 7 minutes.

9. Take out the muffin pans from the oven and let them cool in the pan for 5 to 6 minutes.

10. Remove the muffins from the pan and cool on a cooling rack.

11. Store in an airtight container in the fridge. It can last for 6 - 7 days. You can wrap individual muffins in cling wrap and freeze them.

12. Warm slightly in the microwave and serve.

Double Chocolate Sourdough Bread

Instead of throwing off sourdough discard, you can use it in making other recipes like pancakes, double chocolate sourdough bread, scones, granola bars, etc.

Makes: 2 loaves

Ingredients:

- 3 cups all-purpose flour
- 1 teaspoon salt
- 1 teaspoon baking soda
- 1 teaspoon baking powder
- 1 cup cocoa powder, unsweetened
- 12 tablespoons butter, softened
- 4 eggs
- ½ cup chocolate chips
- 2 cups sourdough starter discard
- 1 ½ cups granulated sugar

Directions:

1.   If you do not have 2 cups of sourdough starter, discard, add some milk to make it 2 cups, and stir.

2.   Preheat your oven to 350°F. Take two loaf pans of 9 x 5 inches each and spray some cooking spray in it.

3.   Place butter and sugar in a mixing bowl. Set the electric hand mixer on medium speed and beat until creamy.

4.   Add eggs, one at a time, and beat well each time.

5.   Mix all dry ingredients in another bowl, i.e., cocoa powder, all-purpose flour, baking powder, and baking soda.

6.   Set the mixer on low speed. Add 1/3 cup mixture of dry ingredients at a time along with ¼ cup sourdough starter, discard and beat until just incorporated each time.

7.   Divide the batter into the loaf pans. Sprinkle chocolate chips on top. Press lightly to adhere. Place loaf pans in the oven and bake for around 45 minutes. To check if the bread is done, insert a toothpick in the center of the loaf and remove it. If you find any particles stuck on it, bake for another 5 - 10 minutes.

8.   Cool for some time before slicing.

Troubleshooting Tips

Sourdough is sometimes quite daunting, even if you are experienced. This is because there is so much involved in it, and you are not expected to get it right on your first go - or even the next few. Here, we'll talk about some of the problems you might experience along the way and how to fix them.

Sourdough Starter

Because the starter is a fermented culture, bringing it to life is not a quick job. While you may see bubbles in the first few days, it isn't unusual for it to go flat a week after you created it. Don't be disheartened - it does take time to get it right.

One of the main reasons this might happen is because your ambient room temperature is not correct. Sourdough starter is a live culture, and it requires the right temperature. Too cool, and the starter is sluggish. Too warm, and it could be overactive and not such a sour flavor.

Test your fed starter in several spots around the house until you find where it is happiest. You will know this because it will rise, fluffy, light, and bubbly, with a melted marshmallow-like texture, within 5 to 8 hours of you feeding it.

Slow-Rising Dough

If your dough isn't rising as fast as it should be, it could be down to two things. The first is the temperature. If you have a cool or drafty house, the dough won't rise as fast as in a warm, draft-free area.

The second reason is down to the dough additions. Your bread will not rise so fast if you use eggs, butter, milk, or a vegan counterpart.

First, ensure your dough is in a warm, not hot, spot, with no drafts and a steady temperature. If you make additions to your dough, make sure they are at room temperature before you add them – if you use them straight from the refrigerator, they will cool the dough temperature and slow down the rising time.

Proofing

Proofing refers to how long the dough rises before it is baked.

If you don't give your dough enough time to rise, your loaf will be under-proofed. While under-proofed dough can rise perfectly well, you may get a tight crumb rather than an airy, open one. It may also be dense and gummy inside when you slice the bread, and you risk large air pockets in the baked loaf. The only way to fix this is to let the dough proof for longer.

If you leave your dough to rise for too long, it becomes over-proofed. This results in the dough being a large puffy ball, and it won't rise when it bakes. Once baked, the crust will be pale, and it will have an unpleasant over-sour taste. To fix this, reduce the rising time by a minimum of an hour.

Stickiness/Sticking

You can't get away from this – the sourdough dough is very sticky. The best way to handle it is to wet your hands lightly with water rather than using flour. If your loaves stick to the pot after shaping, use regular flour, rice flour, or corn flour to dust the pot first, or line it with a clean kitchen towel. When you remove it before baking, tap the excess flour out of the pot but do NOT wash it. Store it somewhere cool and dry, covered to keep it dust-free. Over time, the flour residue will build up lightly, helping reduce sticking.

Scoring/Slashing

Are you struggling to get a nice cut on your loaf? There are three main reasons why this might happen:

Your bread's outer surface is slack and didn't get enough tension when you shaped it. You will know if this is the reason because your knife blade will feel like it is dragging rather than slicing cleanly through the dough.

You are using a blunt knife blade. Make sure you use a sharp blade and, if unsure, choose a different knife before you start.

Your cut wasn't deep enough. You should be able to score the dough cleanly without the dough trying to reattach itself.

• Your Bread Bursts Through the Score

This could happen if your dough were over-proofed, and the only way to prevent it is to reduce how long the dough is bulk-fermented.

• Crust Problems

There are a couple of problems you may encounter with your crust. First, it may be too dark or too light. The easiest way to fix this is to adjust your baking time – longer if it is pale, shorter if too dark. Keep the Dutch oven pot uncovered.

Second, the base of your loaf may be thick, dark, and tough to slice. This happens to experienced bakers as well as beginners, and one way to prevent it from happening is to place a metal baking sheet or pizza stone on the rack underneath the oven. This will absorb heat and stop your bread base from getting tough and dark.

Chapter Six: Kimchi Basics

Kimchi is a delicious Korean dish of fermented vegetables. While there are hundreds of different types of kimchi, the most common one is Napa cabbage kimchi. Like most fermented foods, like yogurt, sauerkraut, or wine, kimchi results from a special fermentation process. The bacteria responsible for it can be found everywhere – in the air, on your body, in vegetable skins, not to mention mammal milk so, if you were breastfed as a child, you received some of that beneficial, healthy bacteria.

So, what is this bacteria?

It's good old-fashioned lactic acid bacteria, which is why the special fermentation is called Lacto-fermentation. The bacteria breaks the large flavor compounds down during the fermentation process, which refines the flavor molecules we can taste.

How Does This Happen?

Lacto-fermentation turns vegetables into kimchi by metabolizing the sugars and carbohydrates in the vegetables into lactic acid. This process gives fermented food a sour taste and an increased acidity level, which, in turn, ensures they are safe to eat.

You might think this is much the same as what causes food to rot, so what is the difference? We can think of the difference between fermentation and rotting as an analogy between two parties.

The rotting party is where everyone can get it – the fungi and the bacteria, the safe and unsafe, the destructive and the flavor-enhancing. The fermentation party has a bouncer that keeps the unwanted "guests" out, only allowing the preferable guests in to make the party go with a bang.

Keeping this firmly in mind, the fermentation process is broken down into three separate stages:

1. The Bouncer – Brine

The first stage of the Lacto-fermentation process is to submerge the vegetables in a brine solution. This is the bouncer, the part that keeps the harmful pathogens out, like Salmonella – these pathogens cannot stand salt because the salt gets in through the cell walls and kills the pathogen. But lactic-acid bacteria is tough, and it survives the salt.

Lactic acid bacteria are anaerobic too, and they can survive without oxygen. When you submerge your vegetables in a brine solution, all the pathogens that love oxygen are eliminated, ensuring they can't spoil the party and make the preferred guests moldy, not safe to eat.

2. The Acid High

As the lactic-acid bacteria settles into the brine, it begins to weave its spells, consuming the carbohydrates and sugar in the vegetables, resulting in the lactic acid. This acid reduces the ferment's pH value, creating an extremely hostile environment, preventing further pathogens from growing, such as botulism (c. botulinum).

Aside from lactic acid, Lactic acid bacteria produces a second by-product, CO_2, better known as carbon dioxide. This is what gives your kimchi its pop when the jar is first opened and gives it a fizzy kick. CO_2 creates a buildup of pressure in your jar, so you must 'burp' the kimchi now and again to stop leakage. Just take off the lid for a second and then replace it.

3. The After-Party

Kimchi doesn't go bad because the fermentation process has broken down the minerals and nutrients, allowing our bodies to absorb them much better. The lactic acid bacteria carries on metabolizing the sugar until it's all gone and, at that point, the kimchi will become vinegar – hint, it can take years! Keep your kimchi in the refrigerator, as this will slow the process. You can use old kimchi in stews and soups, and the juice works well in a Caesar cocktail!

Here's how to make basic cabbage kimchi:

Equipment Required:

- Large colander
- 2 large bowls or pots
- Large glass jar
- Gloves
- Fermentation weights

Traditional Kimchi

Makes: About 1 ½ quart

Ingredients:

- 2 medium heads Chinese Napa cabbage
- Filtered water (non-chlorinated), as required
- 2 teaspoons grated ginger
- 4 to 6 tablespoons fish sauce
- 16 ounces Korean radish or daikon, and cut into matchsticks
- ½ cup kosher salt or sea salt
- 3 tablespoons grated garlic

- 2 teaspoons sugar
- 2 to 10 tablespoons Gochugaru (Korean red pepper flakes) or as per your taste
- 8 scallions, trimmed, cut into 1-inch pieces

Directions:

1. Cut the cabbage in half, halfway through with a knife, starting from the stem side. Separate the two halves with your hands. Do this with both the cabbages.

2. Similarly, cut each half into 2, halfway through with a knife. Separate each into 2 parts with your hands. Discard the core.

3. Now, cut cabbage into about 2-inch cubes.

4. Place the cabbage in a large bowl.

5. Sprinkle salt over the cabbage.

6. Using your hands, mix the salt into the cabbage, massaging the cabbage until it softens a bit.

7. Add water to cover the cabbage.

8. Place a weighted plate over the cabbage to keep it submerged in the solution.

9. Keep aside for about 1 to 2 hours. Place the colander over a bowl and drain the cabbage. Set aside the brine.

10. Rinse the cabbage thrice with cold water. Let the cabbage remain in the colander after the third rinse for 20 – 30 minutes.

11. Meanwhile, combine ginger, garlic, fish sauce, and sugar in a bowl. Stir until sugar dissolves completely.

12. Add red pepper flakes and stir until well combined. This is the seasoning mix.

13. Now wear gloves.

14. Combine radish, cabbage, and scallions in a large bowl and mix well. Add seasoning mix and mix well using your hands. Taste and add more salt if required. The mixture should be salty.

15. Transfer the kimchi into a large glass jar. Pour some retained brine into the jar and press the vegetable mixture, so the brine rises above the vegetable. If the brine does not rise, add

some more brine. You should leave at least an inch of headspace on top of the jar.

16. Close the jar and place it on your countertop for 1 - 2 days, depending on the fermentation. If you are happy with the fermentation after a day, store the jar in the fridge, or you can ferment it for another before placing it in the fridge.

17. It should be ready to eat after 7 - 8 days but tastes better after 15 - 20 days. It can last for about 3 - 5 months.

18. When you see fizzing or lots of bubbles, it is time to discard the kimchi.

Don't forget – red pepper flakes are a traditional ingredient in cabbage kimchi, but make sure you only add to your taste – too much and you won't enjoy it; too little, and you won't taste it.

Fruit Kimchi

Makes: 1 jar

Ingredients:

- ½ fresh pineapple, peeled, cored, cut into bite-size cubes
- 4 pears, cored, chopped, cut into bite-size cubes
- 2 small bunches of grapes, stemmed, halved if desired
- 2 apples peeled, cored, cut into bite-size cubes
- 4 plums, pitted, cut into bite-size cubes
- Any other fruit of your choice, cut into bite-size pieces
- 1 cup cashews or any other nuts
- Juice of 2 lemons
- 2 – 4 jalapeño peppers, finely chopped
- 2 leeks or onions, finely chopped
- 5 -6 tablespoons grated ginger
- 2 – 3 tablespoons finely grated garlic
- 1 – 2 teaspoons Gochugaru (Korean red pepper flakes) or as per your taste
- ½ cup chopped cilantro
- 3 – 4 teaspoons sea salt

Directions:

1. Combine all the fruits, nuts, lemon juice, cilantro, and spices in a large bowl.

2. Transfer into a glass jar. Press the fruits so that the liquid from the mixture rises above the fruits. If it does not, pour some water. Fasten the lid and keep it on your countertop for about two days.

3. Taste the kimchi after two days. If it is fermented to your liking, transfer it to the fridge.

Kkakdugi (Korean Radish Kimchi)

Makes: 1 jar

Ingredients:

- 3.25 pounds Korean radish or daikon radish, rinsed, scrubbed, cut into ½ inch cubes
- 2 scallions, sliced into 1-inch pieces
- 2 ½ - 3 tablespoons Korean coarse salt

For seasonings:

- 5 - 6 tablespoons Gochugaru (Korean red pepper flakes) or as per your taste
- 1 tablespoon Korean fish sauce or to taste
- ½ teaspoon grated ginger
- 1 ½ tablespoons grated garlic
- 1 tablespoons sugar or to taste
- 1/8 cup finely chopped salted shrimp

Directions:

1. In a large bowl, combine ¼ cup salt and sugar. Add radish and mix well. Set aside on your countertop for an hour.

2. Place radishes in a bowl. Add salt and mix well. Let it rest for 35 - 40 minutes.

3. Drain the radishes in a colander.

4. Transfer the radish into a bowl.

5. To make seasoning mixture: Combine fish sauce, spices, sugar, and salted shrimp in a bowl. Let the mixture rest for 10 minutes.

6. Add the seasoning mixture into the bowl of radishes. Mix well. Taste the mixture; it should be salty. If it is not, add some more fish sauce or salted shrimp.

7. Stir in scallions. Transfer the mixture into a jar, and fasten the lid. Set aside on your countertop for 1 – 2 days to ferment. It depends on the temperature to ferment.

8. Transfer the jar into the fridge. It can be used after 8 – 10 days. It will last for about three months.

Fermentation Temperature

It's worth noting temperature plays an important part in fermentation. Like humans, bacteria have an ideal temperature at which they survive. The warmer the temperature, the more active they are and the faster your kimchi will ferment, but too warm, and things will quickly go wrong. If you live in a colder temperature, bacterial activity isn't so high as in a warmer climate. That's no bad thing because if the temperature is too warm, your kimchi will quickly transform into a bowl of acid soup. Cooler temperatures lead to less activity which means the bacteria have more time to do their work. Warmer temperatures lead to much faster fermentation.

When fermentation is fast, though, it's generally because one strain of lactic acid bacteria is more dominant than the others, and your kimchi may have one sour, flat note. It all comes down to taste – if you like your kimchi more robust and sourer, stick to making it in the summer.

In colder climates, you need to watch the temperature carefully. If it drops to 39°F or lower, the bacteria will take far too long to acidify the food. If the environment isn't acidic enough, you risk mold or yeast forming on the kimchi. Fortunately, you can prevent this by leaving a new fermentation at room temperature for two or three days, giving the bacteria the best chance to thrive before moving it back to the refrigerator.

Proper Storage of Kimchi

Kimchi rarely goes bad because the acidity levels stop bad bacteria from forming. However, there are ways to store it to maximize its lifetime.

- **Vacuum packing** – if you own a vacuum packager, it's a great way of storing kimchi. Keep it in the refrigerator until you are ready to open it. Once open, you should consume it within a week but keep it refrigerated – this stops the cabbage from going soft too quickly.

• **Jars** – make sure your jars are sterilized thoroughly before you use them, even brand new ones. Also, make sure the equipment you use to make the kimchi is sterilized before use. Submerge the vegetables completely in the kimchi liquid, or mold can grow. If there is insufficient liquid in the jar to do this, add some more seasoning mix or put a weight on the vegetables to keep them submerged.

Freezing is not recommended because it can kill off probiotics and beneficial enzymes, turning your kimchi bad and uneatable.

Chapter Seven: Sauerkraut for Beginners

Sauerkraut is one of the most popular fermenting projects, and there is a good reason for this – it is dead simple to make, doesn't require much equipment, and tastes delicious. All you do is add salt to shredded cabbage and pack it into a jar or crock. The cabbage will gradually release liquid which, when it mixes with the salt, creates brine. When the cabbage is submerged in this liquid for several days or weeks, it will ferment into the delicious sauerkraut we all know and love.

How Is It Fermented?

In the same way kimchi ferments, sauerkraut ferments by way of lacto-fermentation. The surface of the cabbage contains beneficial bacteria, the same as you find in cultured products such as yogurt. When the bacteria are submerged in the brine, they start to convert the sugars from the vegetable into lactic acid, the natural preservative that stops harmful bacteria in its tracks.

Lacto-fermentation is a centuries-old technique used for preserving seasonal vegetables, thus extending their shelf life. Provided it is done right, it is a safe and reliable method, and you can store your sauerkraut for months in a cellar, at temperatures of around 55°F, or you can store it in your refrigerator.

What Do I Need?

Making basic sauerkraut requires nothing more than cabbage, salt, and a container to ferment it in. One of the most important things to remember is to keep the cabbage submerged in the brine during the fermentation process. If you make large quantities in a crockpot, you should place a heavy plate or weight of some kind over the cabbage to keep it submerged and packed down. If you use a mason jar, place a small jelly jar filled with marbles, rocks, or other weights, into the mason jar's mouth to do the same thing.

Something else to be aware of is the top cabbage will float so, if you are using a mason jar, you will need to tamp the cabbage down a couple of times every day or put a sizeable raw cabbage leaf over the top to hold it down. You should also use cheesecloth or another clean cloth to cover the jar, ensuring dust and insects are kept out, but the air can still flow.

Containers

The most common containers used for fermenting sauerkraut are stone crocks, glass jars, and containers made from food-grade plastic. If you are making large amounts, you can even use five-gallon plastic buckets. You must NOT use galvanized metal, iron, or copper containers or a crockpot glazed with lead. If you are unsure if your container is suitable, use a food-grade plastic bag to line the container with something like a turkey roasting or brining bag. Never use trash liners or garbage bags. No matter what container you use, you must ensure it is sterilized before use as it may contain bad bacteria that interfere with the fermentation process.

Fermentation Time, Temperature and Management

While your sauerkraut is fermenting, keep the container stored at 70 to 75°F. This temperature ensures it takes about three to four weeks to complete the fermentation. If the temperature is 60 to 65°F, it will take longer than six weeks. Above 80°F, the cabbage will soften and spoil, and below 60°F, it will not ferment.

One of the most critical things to remember is following the exact ratios. Five pounds of cabbage requires exactly three tablespoons of salt to control the growth of pathogens. If you change the ratio, you could end up with a product not safe to eat.

The fermentation process will stop naturally when the acids have accumulated to a level where no more growth can occur. Once the cabbage is submerged in the brine, the container must not be disturbed until the fermentation has finished – the bubbling will stop. If you use jars as weights, ensure you check it two or three times a week and spoon off any scum formed on it.

Ideally, your sauerkraut should be tart and firm. The brine must not be cloudy or have any signs of yeast or mold growth. If you see any mold in or on the brine, it smells bad or is slimy, do NOT taste it.

Once your sauerkraut is fermented, you can store it for several months in the refrigerator.

Let's make some sauerkraut.

Equipment Required:

- Large bowl
- 1 glass jar or wide-mouthed plastic container
- Fermentation weights
- Slicer

Cabbage Sauerkraut

Makes: 1 jar

Ingredients:

- 1 tablespoon kosher salt for every 1 ¾ pounds cabbage
- 1 large head of green cabbage (about 4 – 5 pounds) or use as much as required

Directions:

1. Take out a few of the outer leaves of the cabbage and set them aside.

2. Quarter the cabbage first. Cut the cabbage into thin slices using a slicer. You can also slice with a sharp knife.

3. Measure out salt according to the weight of the cabbage. If your cabbage weighs 1 ¾ pound, you then need to use 1 tablespoon of salt.

4. Add salt and cabbage into a large bowl and toss well. Massage the cabbage using your hands for about 8 – 10 minutes. The cabbage will start getting softer, and it will release water.

5. Add the flavorings if using and mix well.

6. Transfer the cabbage into a jar. Press the cabbage down using your hands or spoon so the liquid comes up. Place 2 – 3 of the retained large, outer cabbage leaves on top of the sliced cabbage and place the fermentation weight on the cabbage leaves if necessary.

7. Keep the jar covered loosely with the lid. Set the jar aside for 24 hours, at a temperature of about 65 to 75°F, and it should be away from direct sunlight.

8. Press the cabbage every 2 hours or so. The cabbage should sink in the liquid.

9. Once 24 hours have passed, check for the liquid in the jar. If it is not over the cabbage, combine 2 cups water 2 two teaspoons salt in a bowl and pour as much as required to keep the cabbage below the water level. Generally, enough liquid is there in the jar, and it may not be needed to add some more brine.

10. Cover it loosely and ferment for 7 - 28 days. Make sure there is no sunlight falling on the jar.

11. Taste the sauerkraut daily, from the 7th day. When you are happy with the fermentation, remove the fermentation weights. Fasten the lid.

12. Transfer the jar into the fridge. It can last for 4 - 5 months.

13. Whenever you want to remove sauerkraut, remove it with wooden tongs.

14. If you see any scum or mold floating, it is time to discard the sauerkraut.

Ideas for Different Flavored Sauerkraut

Add the flavorings in step 5 in the sauerkraut recipe. Choose any flavorings of your choice. The flavoring of sauerkraut is optional.

Garlicky Carrots

Ingredients:

- 6 cloves garlic, minced
- 4 carrots, peeled, shredded

Dill Flavor

Ingredients:

- 1 cup fresh dill
- 1 tablespoon caraway seeds (optional)

Ginger and Carrots

Ingredients:

- 2 tablespoons freshly grated ginger
- 4 carrots, peeled, grated

Spicy Beets

Ingredients:

- 2 medium beets, peeled, grated
- 2 teaspoons caraway seeds or ground cinnamon
- 4 cloves garlic, minced

Turmeric Flavor

Ingredients:

- 4 carrots, peeled, grated
- 1 large beet, peeled, grated
- 1 cup grated radish

- 8 cloves garlic, peeled, minced
- 1/3 cup grated fresh turmeric
- 1/3 cup grated fresh ginger

Kimchi Flavor

Ingredients:

- 6 scallions, or green onions, thinly sliced
- 2 carrots, peeled, grated
- 1 cup grated radish
- 6 cloves garlic, peeled, minced
- 2 tablespoons grated ginger
- 2 teaspoons red pepper flakes

Chapter Eight: Yogurt Recipes

Do you ever stop to think about how yogurt is made? Have you ever thought about making your own yogurt?

Most yogurt contains live cultures, which means, yes, your yogurt has living bacteria in it. Before you spit it out in horror, *stop!* These bacteria are healthy and cannot cause you to fall ill. Instead, they turn milk into a creamy, delicious yogurt through a fermentation process.

Fermentation happens when microorganisms break complex substances down into simpler ones, changing the characteristics of your food – grape to wine, milk to yogurt, and so on. These microorganisms are known as "ferments" and are typically yeast or bacteria. They get their energy to grow and develop through the fermentation process.

The Science of Yogurt Fermentation

When one strain of bacteria grows, it typically stops any other from growing. This is because they are all after the same nutrients. However, when you make yogurt, something different happens – two bacteria assist each other in their growth until a stable balance is reached. Those bacteria are Lactobacillus delbruekii ssp. bulgaricus and Streptococcus thermophilus; they work together to turn the lactose in milk into lactic acid. Thus, yogurt is created.

S. thermophilus is much better at growing in high-oxygen, neutral environments, such as milk, than Lactobacillus bulgaricus, so it tends to be the first to grow. It uses the oxygen to create new compounds, which, in turn, create the optimal conditions for L. bulgaricus to start metabolizing and growing.

Now, L. bulgaricus takes over, breaking some milk proteins down into amino acids. This ensures the S. thermophilus can easily collect the nutrients needed for its continued growth.

As both bacteria grow, they consume the lactose present in the milk, turning it into lactic acid. The more they consume, the more acidic the milk is and, once it reaches the right acidity, milk proteins, called caseins, begin clumping together. The milk consistency changes, gradually thickening into yogurt. The two bacteria stop any other bacteria from forming, specifically the bad ones that would cause the milk to spoil, which is why fermentation is one of the best ways of conserving food.

Stopping the Process

When the milk has transformed into yogurt and has reached the texture and flavor you want, the process must be stopped. The simplest way to do this is to reduce the temperature, as cooler temperatures inhibit bacterial growth. Maintaining cooler temperatures also ensures your yogurt retains its flavor and texture by stopping it from increasing in acidity.

I shouldn't have to say this, but, as with everything, using the highest-quality ingredients equates to a higher quality of end product. Where you can, use organic, grass-fed milk and make sure you use a starter. You can use shop-bought yogurt as a starter, but you must make sure you only use one with the live cultures mentioned above.

Alternatively, create your own starter – it's easy to do, and it will ensure your yogurt is high quality and tasty.

How to Make a Yogurt Starter

So simple - and it's much tastier and healthier than using shop-bought yogurt!

Ingredients:

- ¾ cup of raw cow milk (grass-fed, organic)
- Cardamom pods
- Glass measuring cup
- Thermometer
- Glass container to store the starter

Instructions:

1. Heat your milk to a temperature of 120°F
2. Pour it into a clean, sterilized container
3. Break a cardamom pod in half and place both in the milk, submerging them completely. If you cannot find the pods, you can use cardamom seeds – 20 is enough. Once the seeds or pods are submerged, leave it – do not stir as this can interfere with the curdling
4. Cover the container with a clean towel or cheesecloth and leave it somewhere warm, around 70°F. It will take around 10 to 14 hours to curdle, so it's probably best done late in the day and left overnight
5. Make sure your starter is curdled correctly – it should have a sweet smell, not pungent or sour, and be thick.
6. Pour it into a bowl through a strainer, removing the pods or seeds
7. Transfer it to another clean and sterilized container with an airtight lid and store it in your refrigerator. It will keep for up to three weeks.

Here's how to make your yogurt:

Equipment Required:

- Canning jars with lid
- Yogurt maker or instant pot or oven light or heating pad
- Fine wire mesh strainer lined with two layers of cheesecloth only for Greek yogurt
- Thermometer
- Saucepan
- Towels

Yogurt

Makes: 4 1/8 cups

Ingredients:

- 2 tablespoons yogurt starter
- 4 cups milk (use whole raw milk if possible)

Directions:

1. To make yogurt with oven light: Pour milk into a saucepan and heat over medium flame. Check the temperature of the milk. Once it touches 180°F, turn off the heat.

a. Pour the milk into a canning jar. Let the temperature of the milk come down to 115°F.

b. Add a yogurt starter into the jar and whisk well. Close the jar. Turn on the oven light and place the jar in the oven, for 12 to 24 hours, until yogurt sets.

c. Once the yogurt sets, place it in the fridge for a few hours until it chills and sets further.

2.   To make the yogurt in an instant pot: Read the instructions manual of the instant pot before using it. Pour milk into the instant pot and select the "Yogurt" button. It should beep and show 'Boil.' The temperature of the milk should be 180°F.

a. Take out the cooking pot. Let the temperature of the milk come down to 115°F.

b. Add a yogurt starter into the jar and whisk well.

c. Place the cooking pot back into the instant pot. Select the "Yogurt" button and set the timer for 8 - 24 hours, depending on how tangy you want the yogurt to be. Make sure you do not set the timer for longer than 24 hours.

d. Once the yogurt sets, place it in the fridge for a few hours until it chills and sets further.

3.   To make yogurt in a yogurt maker: Pour milk into a saucepan and heat over medium flame. Check the temperature of the milk. Once it touches 180°F, turn off the heat.

a. Let the temperature of the milk come down to 115°F.

b. Add a yogurt starter into the jar and whisk well. Pour into the glass jars of the yogurt maker (read the instructions manual on operating the yogurt maker). Put on the timer for 7 - 15 hours, depending on how tangy you want it to be.

4.   To make yogurt using a heating pad: Pour milk into a saucepan and heat over medium flame. Check the temperature of the milk. Once it touches 180°F, turn off the heat.

a. Take a canning jar and pour the milk into the jar. Let the temperature of the milk come down to 115°F.

b. Add a yogurt starter into the jar and whisk well. Do not close the lid.

c. Set your heating pad to medium. Place a towel on it and place the jar with yogurt over the towel. Wrap the jar with towels as well.

d. After an hour, set the heating pad to low, check after 7 - 9 hours if the yogurt is set.

e. Now cover the jar and keep it in the fridge. Chill for a few hours.

5.   How to make Greek yogurt: Take a fine wire mesh strainer and line it with a double layer of cheesecloth. Place the strainer over a bowl. Add yogurt into the strainer. Place the entire

setup, the bowl, and strainer with yogurt in the fridge for 6 - 24 hours, depending on how thick you want the Greek yogurt to be.

a. The liquid collected is called whey. The whey can be used in smoothies, lemonade, drink it as it is, in curries and gravies, as a starter culture for fermenting vegetables, Lacto-fermented drinks, etc.

Tips for Making Homemade Yogurt

1. You can use whatever milk you want, but whole, 2%, or goat's milk are best. The more fat your milk contains, the thicker your yogurt will be.

2. Your first attempt at yogurt will have a tangy taste, regardless of how long it was incubated. There is nothing wrong with it – it's just that your tastebuds need time to adjust from the sweetened yogurts you buy in the grocery store. Give it a little time, and your tastebuds will adjust, and you won't want to go back to store-bought stuff again.

3. If you want your yogurt to be a little sweeter, add a couple of tablespoons of maple syrup and a scraped vanilla bean or vanilla extract. However, be aware that adding any type of sweetener can detract from the yogurt's taste and health properties.

4. If you want to add some fruit, only do it once the yogurt has incubated. If you add it before, the bacteria won't like it and cannot do the job correctly.

5. You can keep the yogurt for up to ten days in the refrigerator.

6. Before adding any fruit or sweeteners, take a few tablespoons of the yogurt and store it separately. This will help you start your next batch of yogurt, especially if you don't have a yogurt starter to hand

Chapter Nine: Turning Milk into Kefir

If you like yogurt, you'll love milk kefir. It's a tangy, thick, creamy yogurt-type drink packed with probiotics, and it's easy to make at home.

So, what is it?

Milk kefir is fermented similarly to yogurt but with one big difference – the milk is not heated and kept warm. Instead, all you need are something called kefir grains. For those of you who are gluten-free, please don't worry – these are not actual grains. Instead, they are small rubbery, knobbly cell structures where the bacteria and yeast responsible for fermenting the kefir live. They are the kefir equivalent of the scoby you use when you make kombucha.

How It Works

It's a simple process. Add a teaspoon of grains to a cup of milk and over it. Leave it for about a day at room temperature, and the yeast and bacteria will go to work, fermenting the milk and turning it into kefir.

When it's done, it should have a consistency similar to buttermilk and taste tangy, like homemade yogurt. All you need to do is strain out the grains for use in the next batch and enjoy your kefir!

Your kefir grains can be used repeatedly, in batch after batch of kefir, so long as they are healthy. How do you keep kefir grains healthy? Easy – just keep making kefir! You can make a batch every 24 hours or so – your kitchen temperature will determine the exact time. Simply place your grains into another cup of milk and repeat the process. As time passes, the grains multiply – discard the extras or, even better, introduce a friend to the benefits of kefir. If you get to a stage where you don't want to make any more kefir for a while, put the grains in a cup of milk and refrigerate it – it won't start to ferment until you remove it and put it somewhere warm.

What Are the Benefits?

Kefir provides many health benefits, the same as any fermented product. It is packed with probiotics, which lead to healthy gut flora and help in healthy digestion. During fermentation, part of the milk structure is changed, making it much easier to digest. Some people who struggle with milk often find kefir is better for them.

What Milk Should You Use?

Kefir grains work better with full-fat cow, goat, or sheep milk. You can use low-fat or 2% milk, but you might find the grains are sluggish, and the milk takes too long to ferment. If so, place them in whole milk to revive them. Pasteurized or raw milk can be used, but do NOT use UHT (ultra-high temperature) pasteurized milk.

For non-dairy kefir, you can use full-fat coconut milk. However, coconut milk doesn't contain the nutrients and proteins found in animal milk, so your grains will lose some of their vitality over time. Use animal milk for a couple of batches to revive them or, if you cannot have any dairy, simply discard them and purchase new ones.

Other plant-based, dairy-free milk, such as almond and soy, cannot be used for making kefir.

What You Can Do With Milk Kefir

Milk kefir is perfectly drinkable on its own, but you can also add it to your lassis, smoothies, or any other drink you would add regular milk or yogurt to. You can also use kefir for baking. Simply replace buttermilk, milk, or yogurt in the recipe with kefir, and it will result in a fantastic baked product.

Is It Safe? Can Anything Go Wrong?

Milk kefir can be dated back thousands of years. Traditionally, it was used to preserve fresh milk to last longer, so, yes, it is safe. The healthy yeast and bacteria in the grains stop unhealthy ones from growing and spoiling the milk when left at room temperature. You know what happens when you leave milk out of the fridge in a warm room – the grains prevent that.

The biggest thing you need to worry about is the room temperature. The kefir grains are happiest at an average of 60 to 90°F. Below that and the grains will be sluggish, even going into hibernation. While the grains are still okay, the kefir will take longer to make. Above, and the milk will spoil quickly, quicker than it can be cultured by the grains. This promotes an unsafe, unhealthy environment, so you need to avoid making the kefir when it is very hot, and air conditioning isn't available.

Lastly, store your kefir in glass jars. Metal containers can cause the grains to weaken and die; however, they are okay when exposed to metal briefly, such as using a metal strainer or metal spoon to stir the kefir.

Where to Get Your Grains

If you know someone who makes kefir, ask them for some grains. They multiply after a time, and most people who make it regularly will have some to spare. If not, purchase them online but only from reputable organic sources.

Time to make some kefir:

Equipment Required:

- Large jug
- Cheesecloth or coffee filters or paper towels
- Wooden or plastic spoon (slotted)
- Wide glass or plastic bowl
- Jar for storing
- Fine mesh strainer (plastic)
- Rubber bands

Milk Kefir

Makes: About 7 ½ cups

Ingredients:

- 8 cups fresh, raw whole cow's milk, non-homogenized, at room temperature
- 2 tablespoons kefir grains

Directions:

1. Rinse the kefir grains with filtered water and place them in a jug.
2. Pour milk into the jug.
3. Cover the mouth of the jar loosely with cheesecloth for 2 – 3 layers of paper towels or coffee filter. Fasten with rubber bands.
4. Store the jar in a warm and dark place (65 – 85°F). It should be ready in 12 hours to 2 days, depending on the temperature of the place. The ready kefir will have a fermented smell and will be thick. It may be a bit separated, smelling tangy.
5. Place a strainer over a plastic or glass bowl. Add kefir into the strainer and strain into the bowl. The kefir grains can be used to make the next batch of kefir. Alternatively, you can rinse the

grains and place them in a bowl of water in the fridge for a few weeks.

6. Add flavorings, if any now, and stir.

7. Pour the strained kefir into a jar. Seal the jar and chill until use. Consume within two weeks.

Different Flavored Kefir

Flavors are to be added into the prepared kefir after straining and before storing. You can add fresh fruit juice, vanilla extract, dates, cocoa, carob, or any preserved or pureed fruits. The possibilities are endless. Mix and match until you find a favorite. Here are a few ideas.

Fruit Juice

Ingredients:

- 1 tablespoon fresh fruit juice of your choice for every cup of kefir or add more to taste

Flavoring with Extracts

Ingredients:

- 2 cups milk kefir
- ½ to 2/3 teaspoon pure vanilla extract or almond extract
- 2 teaspoons sugar or honey or maple syrup or stevia to taste

Cocoa / Carob

Ingredients:

- 2 cups cocoa powder or carob or 1 – 2 tablespoons Nutella
- 2 cups milk kefir

Fruit Preserve

Ingredients:

- 2 tablespoons fruit preserve of your choice
- 2 cups milk kefir

Fresh Fruit

Ingredients:

- ½ cup chopped fruit of your choice
- 2 cups milk kefir

- 2 teaspoons sugar or honey or maple syrup or stevia to taste

Citrus Strawberry

Ingredients:

- 2 handfuls of fresh or frozen strawberries
- 2 cups milk kefir
- 2 teaspoons lemon juice or lime juice or 2 tablespoons orange juice

Directions:

1. Place strawberries and lemon juice in a blender and blend until smooth. Add to the kefir after straining.

2. You can go for an all citrus flavor by adding a teaspoon of lemon juice, a teaspoon of lime juice, and 2 tablespoons of orange juice.

Banana Berry Flavor

Ingredients:

- 1 cup frozen berries of your choice
- ¼ cup shredded coconut
- 3 to 4 tablespoons applesauce
- 2 cups milk kefir
- 1 large banana, sliced
- Honey or sugar to taste (optional)

Directions:

Place berries, coconut applesauce, banana, kefir, and honey in a blender and blend until smooth.

Mango Flavor

Ingredients:

- 2 cups milk kefir
- ½ to 1 cup cubed mango

Directions:

Place mangoes in a blender and blend until smooth. Add to the kefir and stir.

Pina Colada Flavor

Ingredients:

- ½ cup chopped pineapple
- 2 to 4 tablespoons shredded coconut
- 2 cups milk kefir
- 2 teaspoons lime juice

Directions:

Place pineapple, shredded coconut, lime juice, and kefir in a blender and blend until smooth.

Chapter Ten: Making Beet Kvass

Beet kvass has long been known as a wonder drink, heralding from Russia and the Ukraine thousands of years ago. All ranks and members of society drink it, and many people believe it is safer to drink than water. Across the world, ancient cultures dealt with contaminated water by transforming it into beer, wine, and other alcoholic drinks. Still, they created one of the most wonderous infusions in the North, a Lacto-fermented drink laced with numerous health properties. Not only is it incredibly thirst-quenching, but it is also known to help prevent hangovers, help with healthy digestion, and some claim it protects against infectious diseases.

Traditional kvass is made from sourdough-rye bread gone stale, producing a drink that tastes a lot like beer but without the alcohol. However, many people have had to eliminate grains from their diet for one reason and cannot partake of the health-giving drink. But all is not lost. Beet kvass made with sourdough bread may be the most traditional, but it isn't the only variety. Ever-resourceful, Russians will create kvass from just about anything, from raspberries and currants to cherries and lemons. But perhaps the best-known alternative is made from the good old beet.

Beets are one of the world's superfoods, packed with a nutritional unch rivaled by nothing else. Beets offer one of the best sources of potassium, sodium, calcium, phosphorous, iron, niacin, vitamin A, vitamin C, and fiber. And because they are also packed with folate and folic acid, they are perfect for pregnant women and those trying to fall pregnant. And this humblest and easiest to grow of all root vegetables has even been shown to help prevent some cancers, heart disease, and strokes.

Although beets are a nutritional powerhouse straight from the ground, Lacto-fermentation only serves to boost their nutritional value and benefits. By using a traditional preservation method, probiotics are added, and your body can easily absorb the nutrients in the beets. Cooking tends to destroy nutritional benefits in many foods, so keeping your beets raw throughout the entire process is a bonus.

On top of the benefits for pregnant women, beet kvass also has blood and liver cleansing properties that help stop morning sickness in its tracks. Likewise, because the nutrients in beets help play a critical role in assisting cells to function correctly, beet kvass has long been used across Europe to help treat cancer.

Any Lacto-fermented product chelates the body gently, flushing toxins and heavy metals out. Beet kvass is no exception. Recently converted people to the beet kvass craze tell us it's also an excellent heartburn remedy, chronic fatigue remedy, and helps people manage chemical insensitivities, digestive issues, kidney stones, and allergies.

Lastly, it is believed kvass can improve regularity and alkalize the blood.

And that's not all. Some reports say it has been shown to reduce age spots, helps thicken up thinning hair, and makes gray hairs turn dark again.

So, how do we create this God of all drinks? The most basic version of beet kvass requires just three things – beets, salt, and water. The water and salt combine into a brine that pickles the beets. When the process is finished, the brine has turned into kvass. The beet juice saturates the liquid, and the fermentation provides a slight effervescence. However, like anything, the final product's quality is determined entirely by the quality of the ingredients you use.

Organic beets are preferred, but use whatever you can, so long as they are fresh if you can't get organic. And it's up to you whether you peel the beets or not – just make sure you scrub them clean. The beets are chopped into chunks, approximately one to two inches in diameter. Never shred the beets because they are high in sugar and, when you shred them, too much juice goes into the brine solution. Rather than Lacto-fermentation, you get an alcoholic fermentation instead, but don't be afraid to experiment – if you fancy trying your hand at a beet-based alcoholic drink!

Make sure the water you use is chemical-free, especially chlorine. Chemicals are added to tap water to kill bacteria. If you add them to your ferment, you can see what will happen – not only will they stop the bad bacteria, but they will also stop your good bacteria from growing, causing the beets to go rotten. If you cannot source spring or filtered water, boil tap water and leave it out overnight to ensure the chlorine dissipates.

The salt should NOT be regular table salt or iodized. Make sure only to use unrefined pure sea salt because additives can harm your ferment. Read the labels carefully – some salts labeled as pure contain anti-caking agents, which are a most definite no-no for fermented foods.

Sole plays an essential role in Lacto-fermentation – it stops the bad bacteria forming in the ferment. However, if you use too much, your kvass will be undrinkable. You can combat this by adding a fourth ingredient. Reduce how much salt you add and add some fermented whey instead; the whey kicks the fermentation into gear and provides the same protection as salt against harmful microorganisms.

Whey is easy to obtain if you decide to use it. All you need is plain homemade yogurt or kefir and a way to strain it. You can use shop-bought yogurt, but only if it has the live cultures in it. Homemade is best because the process used to make store-bought yogurt shelf-stable often eliminates the live organisms. If you opt for shop-bought, you can test if it is live very easily.

Heat a cup of milk in a pan on the stove, not allowing it to come to a boil. Mix a tablespoon of your yogurt into the milk and leave it somewhere warm overnight or for at least eight hours. If the milk has thickened noticeably, the yogurt is still live.

Line a strainer or colander with a clean towel or a few layers of cheesecloth and stand it over a bowl. Pour the yogurt into the strainer and leave it to drain. Cover the bowl with a plate or pull the cloth up over it – this keeps the dust and insects out of it. You should see a yellow liquid dripping through – that is the whey. When it's drained to your satisfaction, you can use your whey in the kvass.

Let's make kvass:

Equipment Required:

- Large jar with lid
- Fine wire mesh strainer
- Masons jars or bottles to store

Traditional Kvass

Makes: 1 jar

Ingredients:

- 12 cups water + extra if required
- 1 to 1 ½ cups sweetener like brown sugar, sugar, honey birch syrup
- ½ cup raisins (optional)
- 8 to 12 cups toasted, cubed stale bread (about 8 - 12 ounces)
- ¼ to ½ cup sourdough starter
- Herbs or fruit of your choice

Directions:

1. Combine sugar, water, raisins, herbs, or fruits in a pot and place over high heat. Stir often until the sugar dissolves. When it begins to boil, turn off the heat. Let it cool until it is about 85°F.

2. The bread needs to be cubed and toasted until brown but not burnt. This can be done in the oven.

3. Add sourdough starter and bread cubes in a jar. Drizzle the warm mixture over the bread cubes and stir. If the bread is not covered with water, add a little more.

4. Close the jar's lid loosely and place at room temperature for 2 - 7 days to ferment.

5. Start tasting the mixture daily after two days. When the desired fermentation is reached, strain the mixture into a bowl.

6. Pour into a storage jar and refrigerate until use. Consume within 7 – 10 days. It will not last longer than this.

Beet Kvass

Makes: 1 jar

Ingredients:

- 6 large beets, trimmed, scrubbed, cubed
- 4 tablespoons starter culture (basically 2 tablespoons starter culture for every quart of water)
- 2 teaspoons finely ground sea salt or kosher salt
- 8 cups water or more if required

Directions:

1. Do not peel the skin of the beets. Just scrub them.

2. The different starter culture options are whey from yogurt (from making Greek yogurt), ginger bug, kombucha, juice from fermented pickles, or a commercial starter.

3. Add beets into a large jar of about 2 quarts.

4. Add the starter culture and salt into a bowl and whisk well. Add water and stir until well combined.

5. Place beets in the jar. Pour the brine over the beets. Close the lid tightly.

6. Store the jar at room temperature where there is no source of direct sunlight. Allow it to ferment for 3 – 7 days, depending on the weather. Shake the jar 2 to 3 times every day.

7. Open the lid on alternate days. Push the beets down and close the lid tightly again. When the kvass is ready, lots of bubbles will be visible in the jar. The kvass is ready when it has a pleasant, albeit sour taste. Strain and pour into bottles.

8. Place in the fridge until use. It can be served once chilled. Consume within a month.

Lacto Fermented Fruit Kvass

Makes: 1 jar

Ingredients:

- 2 handfuls strawberries or raspberries or blueberries
- 4 organic apples or pears, cored, sliced, peel if desired
- 1 cup whey liquid
- 2 tablespoons grated fresh ginger
- Filtered water, as required

Directions:

1. Add apples or pears, berries, ginger, and whey into a jar. Pour enough water to fill the jar. Leave about 2 inches of headspace in the top of the jar. Cover the top of the jar loosely with a plastic bag. Place a pint-sized jar at the opening of the jar so the fruits are immersed in the liquid. Put a rubber band around the plastic bag to fasten.

2. Store the jar at room temperature without direct light on the jar. Let it ferment for 2 to 3 days. When the kvass is ready, lots of bubbles will be visible in the jar. The kvass is ready when it has a pleasant and slightly sour taste.

3. Strain and pour into bottles.

4. Place in the fridge until use.

5. To serve: If you do not like the strong fermented taste, dilute it with some cold water and serve.

Chapter Eleven: Ferment Your Own Pickles

Before we talk about fermented pickles, you need to know there is a difference between fermenting and pickling. Both are excellent methods of preserving food naturally, producing wonderful results, but how are they different?

Pickling vs. Fermenting

Both provide very different yet equally tasty results, but confusion occurs because of some overlapping areas. The main difference to remember is this – pickling is about soaking food in vinegar, or another acidic liquid, to produce a sour flavor, while fermenting is all about the chemical reaction between natural bacteria and the sugar in the food, with no additional acid needed.

Pickling

With pickling, food is immersed in vinegar or another acidic solution. This solution changes the texture and taste of the food. Heat is also involved in the process, destroying microorganisms and stopping new ones from growing.

The quickest way is quick pickling, where vinegar, salt, sugar, and occasionally herbs and spices are heated in a pan and brought to a boil. This liquid is then poured over the vegetables or fruits, which are left to soak for a period.

While vinegar is a fermentation product, it does not ferment pickled foods because they do not produce the required enzymes and probiotics.

Fermenting

With fermentation, it's all about chemical reactions, and no additional heat or acidic liquid is needed. Indeed, you can ferment foods with nothing more than salt and a container, although it does tend to be a little more involved than that. Fermentation is an older preservation technique than pickling and takes quite a bit longer to achieve. Ultimately, fermentation alters the food's color, texture, and flavor.

Fermenting 101

Vegetables and fruits have natural bacteria that stop other microbes from growing when deprived of air. Those microbes could cause the food to spoil and promote the growth of mold.

The natural bacteria in the vegetables convert sugars and carbohydrates into lactic acid during fermentation, creating the ideal preservation environment. Lacto-fermentation starts when lactobacillus is present and provides fermented foods with their unique sour, tangy taste. But it does more than that. The fermentation process also creates probiotics to help aid digestion and promote healthy gut flora.

Given that fermentation produces acid, you could class homemade fermented vegetables as pickled too.

Keeping Clean

Cleanliness is a critical part of homemade fermented pickles. That includes your hounds, all the equipment you use, your countertops, jars, everything. If not, you could introduce yeast, bacteria, or mold that spoils your food, leading to mushy, slippery, smelly, off-colored pickles.

Ingredients and Recipes

Always follow a recipe *exactly*. Never leave anything out or reduce or increase any ingredients, especially salt, as it creates the right environment for the good bacteria to grow. Seasonings are usually optional. Your pickles should always be fresh, free of disease, unblemished, and, where possible, organic.

Fermentation Environment

Your environment must be suitable for fermentation to be successful. The temperature should be 70 to 75°F, for a three to four-week fermentation time. Any higher, and you risk the pickles spoiling while lower temperatures slow the fermentation or even stop it altogether.

Storage

You can refrigerate fermented pickles for up to six months but do check them weekly and remove any mold or scum starting to form. If you want to store longer than this, consider canning your pickles.

What Type of Cucumbers?

You need to use pickling cucumbers, which are much smaller than normal salad cucumbers, usually four to six inches long. Their skin is bumpy, they have small seeds, and they are crisp in texture, with a light to dark green color. Try to get organic from your local farmer's market and only use good quality cucumbers. They should be roughly all the same size, so they ferment at the same rate.

HERBS AND SPICES YOU CAN USE

While herbs and spices are optional, they do make a lovely addition to your dill pickles.

- Mustard, fennel seeds, peppercorns, allspice, coriander, celery, and dill seeds go wonderfully with dill pickles. You can use the feathery fronds from a fennel plant (not too much) or chilies for an extra kick.
- Garlic - lots of it - and fresh dill
- Grape leaves or bay leaves - to stop their skins from softening, fermented pickles require tannin.

Salt and Water in Fermentation

The salt and water ratio is the most important aspect of fermentation. Getting it right ensures you have the right environment for the healthy bacteria to grow while prohibiting the bad bacteria. You must be precise when you measure your salt and water:

- Too little salt and the bad bacteria will thrive
- Too much salt and all the bacteria may die, including the good ones, which stops fermentation from happening.

A safe ratio is 2.5% brine, which equates to 6 g of salt for every cup of water. This ratio allows you to drink it without it tasting like seawater! However, if you want your brine stronger, you can go up to 3.5%, which is 9 g of salt per cup of water.

Lastly, make sure you use unprocessed sea salt and filtered water with no chlorine in it.

Tips

- If you require more brine, use a ratio of 1 teaspoon of salt per cup of water

- If you are using grape leaves to provide the tannin, lay it against the side of the jar before adding your vegetables and brine

- If you want to use a river stone as a weight in your jar, ensure you place it in boiling water for 20 minutes first to sterilize it.

Time to make some fermented pickles.

Equipment Required:

- Jar or jars
- Fermentation weights*
- Bowl

These are used to weigh the pickles down, so they are submerged fully in the liquid. You can buy fermentation weights or use a small glass jar filled with stones or marbles, a plate, or even a food-grade bag filled with water – do make sure this cannot break, though, or the fermentation environment will change, and your product will spoil.

Garlic and Dill Pickles

Makes: 1 jar

Ingredients:

- 1 pound pickling cucumbers
- 1 teaspoon fine sea salt for every cup of water
- ½ teaspoon fennel seeds
- ½ teaspoon allspice berries
- ½ teaspoon dill seeds
- ½ teaspoon coriander seeds
- ½ teaspoon peppercorns
- ½ teaspoon celery seeds
- ½ teaspoon mustard seeds
- ½ to 1 fresh red chili or dried Arbol chili, sliced
- 3 cups non-chlorinated filtered water
- 4 to 6 cloves garlic, peeled, sliced

- Small handful dill sprigs
- 2 bay leaves

Directions:

1. Make sure the cucumbers are similar in size. Prepare an ice bath and place the cucumbers in it after rinsing. Let it sit for 15 – 20 minutes. This will help the cucumbers remain crisp.

2. Heat about ½ cup of water until warm. Add ½ teaspoon of salt and stir. Let it cool completely. Pour this brine into a bowl with the remaining water and mix well.

3. Place cucumbers in a jar. Sprinkle garlic, dill, all the spices, and bay leaves over the cucumbers.

4. Pour the brine into the jar. The cucumbers should be immersed in the solution. Place some fermentation weights over the cucumbers so they remain submerged in the brine.

5. Close the lid and tighten it a bit but not too tight. Keep a pan underneath the jar to collect any spills. Keep the jar in a cool and dark area without direct sunlight hitting it for three to seven days.

6. Keep a watch on the jar after three days for any bubbles. If you are satisfied with the taste, store the jar in the fridge and continue fermenting for a few more days until you are satisfied with the results. Make sure to taste the pickles daily starting from the third day.

7. If you want more fizzing on the top of the liquid, make sure to tighten the lid fully. Make sure to open the lid once every five to six days to release some of the gas.

Mixed Pickles

Makes: 1 large jar

Ingredients:

- 6 tablespoons sea salt or pickling salt or kosher salt (3 tablespoons salt for every quart of water)
- 2 cups small cauliflower florets
- 2 cups red bell pepper chunks
- 2 cups carrot slices
- 2 cloves garlic, peeled, smashed
- 2 quarts non-chlorinated filtered water
- 1 teaspoon coriander seeds
- 2 bay leaves
- 2 grape leaves (optional but recommended to keep the vegetables crisp)
- ½ teaspoon black peppercorns

Directions:

1. Heat about ½ cup of water until warm. Add salt and stir. Let it cool to room temperature completely. Pour this brine into a bowl with the remaining water and mix well.

2. Place cauliflower, bell pepper, carrot, garlic, spices, and grape leaves in the jar.

3. Pour the brine into the jar. The vegetables should be covered with the liquid, so add more water if required.

4. Close the lid of the jar and tighten it. Place on your countertop for 2 – 3 days. Open the jar daily once to remove any built-up gas. If you see any scum or molds floating on top, remove them with a spoon.

5. If the pickles are to your liking, store the jar in the fridge.

6. It can last for about 1 – 1 ½ months.

Pickled Green Tomatoes

Makes: 1 small jar

Ingredients:

- 2 tablespoons kosher salt
- 4 sprigs dill
- 4 cloves garlic, peeled, sliced ·
- 2 teaspoons coriander seeds
- 4 green tomatoes, thinly sliced
- 2 green onions, thinly sliced
- 2 teaspoons whole black peppercorns
- 4 cups water

Directions:

1. Combine salt and water in a bowl. Keep stirring until salt dissolves completely.

2. Take a jar and keep the tomato slices in it. Sprinkle garlic, peppercorns, coriander seeds, dill, and green onions on top.

3. Pour brine into the jar. The ingredients should be immersed in water. If necessary, place a cabbage leaf on top of the ingredients to keep the ingredients immersed. If necessary, keep something heavy over the leaf.

4. Close the lid and tighten it a bit but not too tight. Keep a pan underneath the jar. This is to collect any spills from the jar. Keep the jar in a cool and dark area without direct sunlight hitting it for 5 - 10 days.

5. Keep a watch on the jar after three days for any bubbles. Continue fermenting until bubbling stops. If, at any time, the liquid seems less in the jar, just stir a bit of salt in some water and pour it into the jar. Now the pickle can be placed in the fridge. It can last for 3 – 4 months.

Granny's Pickle

Makes: 1 jar

Ingredients:

- 2 tablespoons salt for every quart of water
- ½ jar chopped seasonal garden vegetables, cut into bite-size pieces
- 5 – 7 cloves garlic, peeled, sliced
- 1 onion, sliced
- 2 grape leaves or horseradish leaves (optional but recommended to keep the vegetables crisp)
- A handful of herbs of your choice
- ½ teaspoon each - pickling spices of your choice like peppercorns, coriander seeds, etc.
- 1 quart filtered, non-chlorinated water

Directions:

1. Place garlic, pickling spices, and herbs in the jar. Spread vegetables over the spices. Place grape leaves as well. One grape leaf will do. You can also put in a few black tea leaves if you do not have grape leaves or horseradish leaves.

2. Pour water into a bowl. Stir in the salt. Let it dissolve completely.

3. Pour brine into the jar, and the vegetables should be covered with the brine. The ingredients should be immersed in water. Press the vegetables down. If necessary, place a cabbage leaf on top of the ingredients to keep the ingredients immersed. If necessary, keep something heavy over the leaf.

4. Close the lid and tighten it fully. Store the jar in a warm and dark place (65 – 85°F) without direct sunlight for 9 – 10 days. Make sure to loosen the lid once daily, to remove excess gas. Be quick in opening and closing it tightly again.

5. Once you are happy with the taste, store the jar in the fridge.

Turnip Pickle

Makes: 1 jar

Ingredients:

- 1 ¾ tablespoons sea salt
- 3 cups water
- 1 teaspoon red pepper flakes
- 6 medium turnips, scrubbed, cut into 1/8-inch-thick slices

Directions:

1. Combine salt and water in a bowl. Add turnips and red chili flakes into the jar—drizzle brine over the turnips.

2. Keep the jar covered tightly and place at room temperature for 3 - 4 days or until you are satisfied with the fermentation. Open the lid for a few seconds daily to remove excess gas.

3. Store the jar in the fridge. It is ready to eat on the 5th day. It can last for 18 - 20 days.

Indian Vegetable Kanji

Makes: 1 jar

Ingredients:

- 1 pound carrots or radish or black carrots, peeled, sliced
- 3 tablespoons coarsely ground yellow mustard
- 5 - 6 cloves garlic, peeled
- 10 cups water
- 3 tablespoons salt
- 1 teaspoon turmeric powder
- 2 teaspoon red chili flakes

Directions:

1. Combine salt and water in a bowl.

2. Place the chosen vegetable in the jar.

3. Blend garlic, turmeric powder, mustard, and chili flakes, adding a little of the brine in a blender until smooth.

4. Add into the brine and stir. Pour into the jar. Fasten the lid and place it in a warm area for about 3 - 4 days. If you can manage to place it in the sunlight, there is nothing like it. Initially, the vegetables will sink in the brine. As it ferments, it will begin to float. If you cannot place it in sunlight, it will take 5 - 7 days to ferment.

5. Once you are satisfied with the taste, store the jar in the fridge.

Chapter Twelve: How to Make Apple Cider Vinegar (ACV)

When fall arrives, so do the apples, and households everywhere start to smell of apple pies. What do you do with your scraps? The peel, the core, and any other part leftover from baking? Whatever you do, don't throw them away because you can use them to make one of the healthiest ingredients on the planet – raw apple cider vinegar. It's really easy to make, and the benefits are enormous. Oh yeah, and because you are using leftovers, it's far cheaper than buying ACV from a store.

You can find apple cider vinegar all over the place. All grocery stores sell it, and everyone is talking about it. Is it hype? A new fad? Or is there more to ACV than first meets the eye?

I can tell you now, ACV is nothing new. It is one of the world's ancient remedies and has long been used in helping with health issues, but it seems we are only now starting to become more aware of the benefits.

These days, people are more aware of their health and do all they can to improve it by making natural, healthy choices. That is why ACV is seen everywhere and heard in just about every conversation about natural remedies and healthy foods.

And, in case you were wondering, most of the benefits attributed to apple cider vinegar are fully backed by science. So no, it isn't hype, and it isn't another fad.

However, you should note that apple cider vinegar can only do so much, incredible as it is. It isn't a miracle worker, and it doesn't take the place of a healthy, balanced diet and exercise program. Yes, it promotes good health, and it can undoubtedly help you maintain your health, but drinking it won't have a significant impact on your life unless you combine it with other steps towards a healthy life.

What Is Apple Cider Vinegar?

Basically, it is vinegar made from apples, but it's fermented apple juice, to be more specific.

A good apple cider vinegar is not cheap to buy, but you can easily make your own from apples or apple peels and cores. The apples are crushed, exposing them to yeast, and natural sugar found in the apple is fermented into alcohol. It sounds much like making cider, and that's because it's a similar process. The only difference is, to make the vinegar, we ferment it *twice.* The first time makes the cider; the second time makes the vinegar.

Why Drink it?

Apple cider vinegar is classed as a superfood, providing tons of health benefits, which we'll talk about in a minute. It is also an excellent weight-loss tool because it induces satiety, which reduces cravings. And it is packed with tons of nutritional benefits.

The Benefits of Apple Cider Vinegar

So, what are these much-talked-about benefits? We'll start by listing them and then get into the details of the ones that can really help you with a healthy life:

- Apple cider vinegar aids digestion and is a natural laxative

- It helps lower your blood sugar

- It can improve insulin sensitivity

- It helps weight loss by increasing satiety and decreasing cravings

- It can reduce unhealthy belly fat

- It can help lower your cholesterol

- It improves your heart health by lowering blood pressure

- It can decrease the risks of cancer or prevent it altogether and slow cancer cell growth.

Well, all this sounds incredibly impressive, but it doesn't end there. Apple cider vinegar is also packed with nutrients, which goes a long way towards explaining why it has so many health benefits. Here's what ACV contains:

- Amino acids

- Antioxidants

- Iron

- Magnesium

- Manganese

- Phosphorus

And one tablespoon is just three calories.

Let's go deeper into those health benefits:

Weight Loss

Losing weight is the primary reason people use ACV, but many don't realize all the other health benefits it offers. That's mainly because apple cider vinegar has long been used for weight loss. Some studies show it works, too – even if you don't make any changes to your diet. However, combine it with a healthy lifestyle, and the results will blow your mind.

How does this work? The main reason people eat so much is that they don't feel full, and keep right on eating. It takes 20 minutes for your stomach to send a message to your brain saying it is full – you can eat a lot of food in that time! ACV increases satiety, which means you feel full quicker, eat less, and stay on track with a healthy, balanced diet. This is even more important when you are just starting your weight loss journey.

Diabetes

There are several things to know about apple cider vinegar and diabetes, mainly that it is a great tool to help prevent diabetes from starting. If you have a history of diabetes in your family, it may be worth consuming ACV to decrease your risks of getting it.

It works because it reduces blood sugar when you fast (when you don't eat). This is highly beneficial for anyone who struggles to regulate blood sugar, like those with diabetes. However, please do not stop taking medication – ACV cannot replace what your doctor has prescribed.

People with diabetes are urged to eat a healthy diet and exercise as much as they can. If you are on prescription drugs, you must seek advice from your doctor before consuming apple cider vinegar – it may cause a serious drop in potassium levels.

Blood Pressure and Cholesterol

Apple cider vinegar has also been shown to reduce blood pressure and cholesterol, but how? ACV helps to control a hormone called renin; this hormone is produced by the kidneys and helps dilate and constrict blood vessels. When they constrict, blood pressure goes up and, when they dilate, it goes down. ACV helps the vessels to relax, keeping your blood pressure down and stable.

In terms of cholesterol, when you drink ACV before you eat, it can lower your cholesterol levels. The antioxidants in apple cider vinegar help reduce LDL (bad cholesterol) and raise good cholesterol (HDL).

Digestion

Apple cider vinegar has long been shown to improve digestion by eliminating heartburn, reducing bloating, and improving your overall digestive health.

Pain and discomfort are not normal, and when we experience it after eating, we really should listen to what our bodies are telling us – something isn't right. We may have overeaten, or another issue is preventing the digestive system from working correctly.

The digestive system can only work properly when the correct acid levels are in the stomach, helping us absorb the nutrients from what we eat. When there is insufficient acid, the food isn't broken down properly, and the nutrients are not absorbed, leading to the digestive issues mentioned above or, in some cases, something much worse. When you drink apple cider vinegar, you increase acid production in the stomach, leading to your digestive system working as it should.

Bacteria

Apple cider vinegar will kill bacteria, and in earlier times, it was used to disinfect wounds and kill fungus. It still is a good way of treating infections because of its ability to kill bacteria. It will also stop E-coli, and other bad bacteria, from spoiling your food, which is why ACV is often used to preserve food naturally rather than using artificial preservatives.

Cancer

While it isn't clear exactly how it works because apple cider vinegar promotes health, it is thought to help prevent cancer. While it isn't a cure, and we know we have a long way to cure and prevent cancer, it has been shown to reduce the risks of getting it when combined with a healthy lifestyle. It has also been shown to slow down the growth of cancerous cells and tumors.

However, I must stress that remedies such as ACV should never be used to replace treatment in someone who has been diagnosed with cancer. Nor should it replace a healthy lifestyle for people wanting to reduce the risks of cancer. It is an addition, a supplement if you like, but if you are on any prescription drugs or treatment, you must seek advice from your doctor before using ACV.

Hair and Skin

Apple cider vinegar doesn't just have health benefits. It can also improve your hair and skin health, and here's how:

- It can treat existing acne and reduce the frequency of outbreaks
- It can soothe and treat sunburn
- It contains anti-aging properties
- It can improve your hair health
- It can combat tangles in your hair
- It can reduce frizziness
- It can seal off the hair cuticles, helping your hair to retain natural oils and moisture

• It can treat dandruff

However, while it has all these wonderful properties, there is one thing I must tell you - never apply neat ACV to your skin. It must be diluted in water first.

Best Ways to Consume Apple Cider Vinegar

With all its many benefits, you may be reaching for a bottle right now, preparing to take a swig. First, we'll look at the many other ways you can consume your freshly made ACV:

> • Drink it but not neat - if you like the taste, go for it but don't down half the bottle in one go! A tablespoon or two is more than enough, mixed into a glass of water.

> • Use it in your recipes - later, I will provide you with a couple of excellent salad dressing and marinade recipes you can use it in.

> • Make a tonic - mix two tablespoons of ACV into a glass of fruit juice. This way, you still get all the benefits without the taste - along with the benefits of the fruit juice (make sure it is pure with no added sugars, flavorings, etc.) Add a touch of cayenne pepper or ground cinnamon to spice it up or a dash of raw honey to sweeten it.

How Much to Drink Every Day

This is a critical point - overdoing it will NOT increase the benefits and can cause you additional health problems. Don't forget - *ACV is acidic.*

The ideal dosage is 15 to 30 ml per day - one or two tablespoons, that's all. If you have never consumed ACV before, start with one tablespoon diluted in a cup or two of water. It is strong so give yourself time to get used to it. From there, you can increase the amount of vinegar.

Potential Side Effects

It is only vinegar made from apples, so, used in moderation, it is perfectly harmless. However, drink too much, and you invite problems. Plus, if you have kidney disease, other issues with your kidneys, or stomach ulcers, steer clear – it is far too acidic and can worsen some health problems. Always seek advice from your doctor first.

Just to remind you – always dilute ACV in some way before consuming it, be it in water, marinades, salad dressings, juices, etc. drinking neat ACV or too much of it can:

- Strip the enamel from your teeth and cause tooth decay
- Lower your potassium levels. If you already have low potassium, do not consume more than the recommended daily allowance
- Cause indigestion if you drink too much
- Cause worsening digestion issues in those with acid reflux or stomach ulcers
- Burn your skin if applied undiluted. For sunburn, add two tablespoons of ACV to your bath and, for acne, dilute a tiny bit in water before you apply it.

As with many things, a little bit of apple cider vinegar can go a very long way – moderation is key!

Let's make our first batch of ACV.

Equipment Required:

- Large jar (2-quart size)
- Smaller jar
- Cheesecloth or coffee filter
- Rubber band
- Fermentation weights

ACV Recipe

Ingredients:

- 1 tablespoon cane sugar for every cup of water
- Organic apple scraps (chopped whole apples, peels, cores, etc.) preferably from a variety of apples
- 4 cups filtered water or more if required

Directions:

1. Make sure your jar is clean and dry.
2. Place apple scrap in a 2-quart jar, enough to fill up to ¾.
3. Combine water and sugar in a saucepan. Stir until sugar has completely dissolved.
4. Pour the sugar solution into the jar. Press the apples until they are immersed in the sugar solution.
5. Despite pressing, if the solution is not over the apples, dissolve 1 – 2 tablespoons of cane sugar in 1 – 2 cups of water and pour into the jar.
6. Place some fermentation weights over the apples to keep them submerged in the sugar solution.
7. Keep the jar covered with cheesecloth and fasten it with a rubber band. Store the jar in a dark place at room temperature for approximately three weeks. Keep a watch over it and check for any mold growth. If you find some mold, remove it.
8. By now, you should be getting a slightly sweet smell.
9. Strain the liquid into another jar. Press the apples to extract as much liquid as possible. Discard the solids.
10. Cover with another cheesecloth and fasten with a rubber band. Store the jar in a dark place at room temperature for approximately 3 – 4 weeks.
11. Stir the vinegar every 4 – 5 days and taste it as well. When you are happy with the taste, remove the cheesecloth and put the lid on.

12. Remove a little of the vinegar floating on top (this is called "the mother") and store it for whenever you make ACV again. When you make a new batch of ACV, add a little of "the mother" so it can speed up the fermentation process.

Apple Cider Vinegar Salad Dressing

Making a salad dressing with ACV takes just five minutes. It's delicious, cheap, and far healthier than what you buy in the shops:

Ingredients:

- 1 small shallot, peeled, cored, and chopped into quarters – if you can only get large ones, just use one lobe
- 1/3 cup extra-virgin olive oil
- 2 teaspoons honey
- 2 teaspoons Dijon mustard
- ½ teaspoon sea salt
- ¼ teaspoon ground black pepper

Instructions:

1. Put all the ingredients into a blender, mini chopper, or a jug with an immersion blender
2. Blitz to a smooth puree – it should take about 30 seconds
3. Use immediately or refrigerate in a sealed container for up to one week.

Notes

You can make this ahead and store it, but it will solidify after a couple of days. Remove it from the refrigerator and bring it to room temperature before using it. If you need it straight away, place the jar in a bowl of warm – not boiling – water.

Apple Cider Vinegar Marinade for Chicken

This marinade is simple to make, taking just five minutes, and can be used for any meat, poultry, or fish.

Ingredients:

- 2 lbs. boneless, skinless chicken breast
- 1/3 cup extra-virgin olive oil
- ¼ cup fresh lemon juice
- 3 tablespoons apple cider vinegar
- 3 cloves garlic, pressed
- ¼ cup fresh chopped basil
- ¼ cup fresh chopped parsley
- 1 teaspoon fresh chopped rosemary
- 1 teaspoon fresh chopped thyme
- ½ teaspoon sea salt
- ½ teaspoon ground black pepper

Instructions:

1. Place all the ingredients in a bowl and whisk until combined
2. Poke the chicken (or whatever meat or fish you are using) with a fork all over and place in a dish or Ziploc bag
3. Pour the marinade in and cover the meat completely
4. If using a dish, cover with plastic wrap and marinate for between 30 minutes and four hours, depending on your taste
5. Use in your recipe

Apple Cider Vinegar Marinade for Pork

Again, this marinade can be used for any meat or poultry and takes just five minutes to prepare.

Ingredients:

- ½ cup of fresh apple cider
- ¼ cup extra-virgin olive oil
- ¼ cup fresh apple cider vinegar
- ½ teaspoon garlic powder
- ¼ teaspoon mustard powder
- 1 tablespoon light brown cane sugar or Demerara
- 1 teaspoon sea salt
- 1 tablespoon raw honey
- 1/8 teaspoon ground coriander or 1/3 teaspoon finely chopped fresh

Instructions:

1. Place all the ingredients in a medium bowl and whisk until combined

2. Place your pork chops in a Ziploc bag and pour the marinade in. Make sure the meat is completely covered and then seal the bag, removing the air

3. Marinate for between eight hours and a day before cooking

This makes enough for about two or three medium pork chops – if you need more, adjust the recipe accordingly.

Quick Tips

When you make your apple cider vinegar:

- Try to use organic fruit, free of chemicals
- Do not use fruit with any mold, soft spots, signs of rot, or fungi
- Rinse your apples under cold running water before using them
- If you are making your vinegar from whole apples, they should be soaked in a bowl of water first. Add a tablespoon of ACV to the water and leave them for five minutes. This simple addition will kill any bacteria, and if you can't source organic apples, it will also remove chemical residues.

Conclusion

Now that we have reached the end of the book, I am sure you have all the information you need to start fermenting. Many people across the globe have taken to fermentation and have started drinking kombucha and eating kimchi to clear their gut. If you want to do the same, then use this book as your ultimate guide.

You now know that fermentation is the process of breaking down carbohydrates in foods into organic acids and alcohol using microorganisms, such as bacteria and yeast. This process only works if you have good bacteria in the mix since they can break the sugars and starch in food down easily. These microorganisms grow in number, and as they divide, they form lactic acid, preventing the growth of harmful bacteria in the food. The fermented food you end up eating has an acidic or tangy taste because of the lactic acid.

You can store fermented food for a long time. You can keep it for years as long as you store it in a dark and cool place. It is also essential to keep these foods in brine (a mixture of salt and water). Use the methods mentioned in the book to get started with fermenting. Once you finish the fermentation process, transfer the food to a cold storage area. You can store the food in a cold cellar or fridge, but make sure you maintain the temperature between 32 and 50 degrees. Do not use an airlock but a regular lid. The cold temperature will slow down the organisms' growth, which helps preserve the food while it continues to age. If you ferment vegetables, you can store them for a year. Consume fermented fruit within a week or a month at most to avoid alcohol formation.

It is okay to freeze any food you ferment, as well. This means the organisms stop growing altogether, which increases the shelf life of the fermented product. Make sure you double or even triple-layer the food to prevent freezer burns. Bear in mind that you need to follow the measurements given in the book to a tee. If you do not stick to these measurements, you may mess with the growth of the microorganisms. The book has everything you might need. Use this book as your guide. The recipes in this book are very straightforward and relatively easy to follow, and you can tweak them to suit your tastes. Few people will like the taste, but if you do, give these recipes a shot.

You will probably make some mistakes here and there, but this is normal. Learn from your mistakes and make sure you try new things. You will learn and get to the point where fermenting becomes just as easy as cooking.

Happy fermenting!

Here's another book by Dion Rosser that you might like

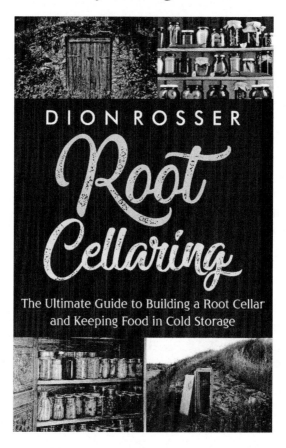

Resources

Bilodeau, K. (2018, May 16). Fermented foods for better gut health - Harvard Health Blog. Harvard Health Blog. https://www.health.harvard.edu/blog/fermented-foods-for-better-gut-health-2018051613841

Clime, K. (2014). Beyond Sauerkraut: A Brief History of Fermented Foods. Lhf.org. https://www.lhf.org/2014/03/beyond-sauerkraut-a-brief-history-of-fermented-foods/

Coyle, D. (2019, January 15). What Is Fermentation? The Lowdown on Fermented Foods. Healthline; Healthline Media. https://www.healthline.com/nutrition/fermentation#benefits

Delany, A. (2018, January 29). 13 Fermenting Supplies to Buy Online Before You Start Making Kombucha or Whatever. Bon Appétit. https://www.bonappetit.com/story/fermenting-supplies-online

Fermentation: A History. (2017, December 8). EatCultured. https://eatcultured.com/blogs/our-awesome-blog/fermentation-a-history

Fermentation Supplies. (N.d.). Grow Organic. https://www.groworganic.com/collections/fermentation-supplies

Fermentation Supplies | Jars, Crocks, Pounders, Airlocks, & Kits. (n.d.). Retrieved June 1, 2021, from https://www.culturesforhealth.com/learn/natural-fermentation/fermentation-equipment-choosing-the-right-supplies/

Hooper, C. (2016, April 22). 10 Health Benefits of Fermented Food. Naturalife. https://naturalife.org/nutrition/health-benefits-fermented-food

Howe, H. (2017, January 12). The Best Fermenting Supplies for Sauerkraut & Vegetables. MakeSauerkraut. https://www.makesauerkraut.com/fermenting-supplies/

Kresser, C. (2020, June 25). The 13 Benefits of Fermented Foods and How They Improve Your Health. Chris Kresser. https://chriskresser.com/benefits-of-fermented-foods/

MacCharles, J. (1 C.E., November 30). Fermenting Tools/ Equipment/ Supplies. WellPreserved. https://wellpreserved.ca/fermenting-tools-equipment-supplies/

Marcene, B. (2020, July 9). 12 Amazing Health Benefits of Fermented Foods - Natural Food Series. Natural Food Series; Natural Food Series. https://www.naturalfoodseries.com/12-benefits-fermented-foods/

ResearchGuides: Fermentation Science: History of Fermentation Science. (2019). Lindahall.org. https://libguides.lindahall.org/c.php?g=242326&p=1616528

Shurtleff, W., & Aoyagi, A. (2020). A Brief History of Fermentation, East and West. Soyinfocenter.com. https://www.soyinfocenter.com/HSS/fermentation.php

Tay, A. (2019, July 18). The Science of Fermentation. Lab Manager. https://www.labmanager.com/insights/the-science-of-fermentation-1432

"Beet Kvass: The Miracle of Russia." Homestead.org, 12 June 2020, www.homestead.org/food/beet-kvass-of-russia/.

"How to Make Homemade Sauerkraut in a Mason Jar." Kitchn, Apartment Therapy, LLC., 6 Aug. 2013, www.thekitchn.com/how-to-make-homemade-sauerkraut-in-a-mason-jar-193124.Fermented Dill Pickles Video.

"How to Make Fermented Pickles!" Feasting at Home, 22 Aug. 2019, www.feastingathome.com/fermented-pickles/.

"How Does Kimchi Ferment? The Science of Lacto-Fermentation and Kimchi." Baechu Kimchi, baechukimchi.ca/kimchi-and-lacto-fermentation/.

"How to Make Kombucha." BBC Good Food, www.bbcgoodfood.com/howto/guide/how-make-kombucha."How to Make Milk Kefir." Kitchn, www.thekitchn.com/how-to-make-milk-kefir-cooking-lessons-from-the-kitchn-202022.https://www.facebook.com/asweetpeachef.

"19 Benefits of Drinking Apple Cider Vinegar + How to Drink It." A Sweet Pea Chef, 20 Apr. 2019, www.asweetpeachef.com/benefits-of-apple-cider-vinegar/.Moyano, Carolina.

"The Chemistry behind the Fermentation of Yogurt." Www.foodunfolded.com, 8 July 2020, www.foodunfolded.com/article/the-chemistry-behind-the-fermentation-of-yogurt."Science of Kimchi: What Affects the Taste of Kimchi? Take a Walk on the Wild Side." Baechu Kimchi, baechukimchi.ca/take-a-walk-on-the-wild-side/.

"Sourdough Bread: A Beginner's Guide." The Clever Carrot, 3 Jan. 2014, www.theclevercarrot.com/2014/01/sourdough-bread-a-beginners-guide/."Troubleshooting Sourdough Bread." Baked, 21 Jan. 2021, www.baked-theblog.com/troubleshooting-sourdough-bread/.

"What's the Difference between Pickling and Fermenting?" Kitchn, https://www.thekitchn.com/whats-the-difference-between-pickling-and-fermenting-229536.